"An engaging book . . . When Mr. Bailey was writing this book, he may as well have pinned my photo above his desk and labeled it 'my audience.' . . . *Hyperfocus* helped me recognize the limits of my attentional space and make my environment more conducive to focus. . . . Mr. Bailey teaches how to re-examine your tasks, determine your priorities, and minimize interruptions. . . . When I started the second part of the book, I excitedly placed exclamation points next to all of the examples of places your mind could go if it was left to do its own thing."

—*The New York Times*, Self-Helped column

"Better than coffee . . . In this practical and widely applicable manual Bailey . . . identifies distraction as an endemic problem plaguing the business world, and just about every facet of modern life as well. . . . Highly germane to any fast-paced workplace, this book is a must-read for readers seeking to regain control of their ability to concentrate."

—*Publishers Weekly*

"*Hyperfocus* does a remarkable job of unpacking the realities, obstacles, and best practices of managing the subtle but ever-present world of our conscious attention. All of us can get better at how, when, and on what we focus; and this is an extraordinary, eye-opening, and research-based report of what affects us in this regard, and how to take advantage of this information to achieve greater satisfaction in our lives. Bravo, Chris."

—David Allen, author of *Getting Things Done*

"Becoming more productive isn't about time management; it's about attention management. I'd tell you more about that, but I lost my train of thought. Luckily this attention-grabbing book is here to help. Chris Bailey offers actionable, data-driven insights for sharpening your focus— and finding the right moments to blur it."

—Adam Grant, author of *Originals*, *Give and Take*, and *Option B*

"The best productivity plans call for strategy, not just hacks or tactics—and *Hyperfocus* gives you strategy in spades. When you read this book, get ready to do your most important work!"

—Chris Guillebeau, author of *The $100 Startup*, *The Art of Non-Conformity*, and *The Happiness of Pursuit*

"Let me guess. You're like me. You don't have time to read this book. Or any book! Who has time for books anymore? Well, that's perfect. Because it means you have the disease. And right now you're holding the cure."

—Neil Pasricha, author of *The Book of Awesome* and *The Happiness Equation*

"I read *Hyperfocus* on my phone . . . but this book was so engaging I stopped checking email entirely! I highly recommend this book to anyone looking to do more of what matters in a distracted world."

—Laura Vanderkam, author of *What the Most Successful People Do Before Breakfast*, and *168 Hours*

"There are two kinds of focus we need in order to pursue what's essential in life: focus as a noun (our fixed intent) and focus as a verb (the ongoing process of connecting the dots). This is brilliantly illustrated both in writing and in graphics in this latest book from Chris Bailey. I loved the book."

—Greg McKeown, author of *Essentialism*

"Practical, well written, and timely. Chris Bailey tackles one of the most important topics today as we seek success at work and attempt to raise positive kids in the modern world. What you attend to becomes your reality. *Hyperfocus* provides a practical path to using our attention to create an adaptive reality. If you want to achieve greater success and happiness, we need to start by focusing upon what our brain is attending to."

—Shawn Achor, author of *The Happiness Advantage* and *Big Potential*

"Chris Bailey's book is a fascinating guide to managing our attention. He describes a methodology that will help us both focus and create more effectively. His book is not just theory, but a wonderful toolbox full of practical and detailed best practices. I can't wait to give these ideas a try."
—Kai-Fu Lee, author of *AI Superpowers*, founder of Google China

"*Hyperfocus* is a lifeline in a world in which we are all overwhelmed with too much to do and not enough time to do it Thanks to Chris Bailey's groundbreaking and timely new book, I feel like I now have, for the first time in literally years, the ability to focus on the most important, value-creating things. Read this book if you want a stress-relieving salve as well as a guarantee to improve both your productivity and happiness."
—James M. Citrin, author of *The Career Playbook*

"Being hyperfocused in a busy world is a skill every professional needs in their arsenal. Chris Bailey will show you how to master it in his new book *Hyperfocus*. Using all of the latest science, Bailey gives readers practical, incredible frameworks to change how you work."
—Vanessa Van Edwards, author of *Captivate*

"There's no question: your attention is your most valuable asset. Everything in your life—your experience of life—comes from your attention. And *Hyperfocus* will teach you how to use this tool, how to hone it, leverage it, and even enjoy it. Pay attention to Chris Bailey—this book is well worth the focus."
—Peter Bregman, author of *18 Minutes*

"Attention may be the most important asset of the twenty-first century. *Hyperfocus* takes decades of scientific insights and pairs them with practical application to show us all how best to manage and multiply our attention."
—David Burkus, author of *Under New Management* and *Friend of a Friend*

PENGUIN BOOKS

HYPERFOCUS

Chris Bailey has been intensively researching and experimenting with productivity since he was a young teenager, in an effort to discover how to become as productive as humanly possible. To date, he has written hundreds of articles on the subject, and has garnered coverage in media as diverse as *The New York Times*, *The Wall Street Journal*, *GQ*, *The Huffington Post*, *New York Magazine*, *Harvard Business Review*, *TED*, *Fast Company*, and *Lifehacker*. The author of *The Productivity Project*, Chris lives in Kingston, Canada.

HYPERFOCUS

HOW TO MANAGE
YOUR ATTENTION
IN A WORLD
OF DISTRACTION

CHRIS BAILEY

PENGUIN BOOKS

PENGUIN BOOKS

An imprint of Penguin Random House LLC

penguinrandomhouse.com

First published in the United States of America by Viking,
an imprint of Penguin Random House LLC, 2018
Published in Penguin Books 2019

Illustrations by Chris Bailey and Sinisa Sumina.

ISBN 9780525522256 (paperback)

THE LIBRARY OF CONGRESS HAS CATALOGED THE
HARDCOVER EDITION AS FOLLOWS:

Names: Bailey, Chris, 1989– author.
Title: Hyperfocus : how to be more productive in
a world of distraction / Chris Bailey.
Description: New York : Viking, [2018] | Includes
bibliographical references and index. |
Identifiers: LCCN 2018023750 (print) |
LCCN 2018025476 (ebook) | ISBN 9780525522249 (ebook) |
ISBN 9780525522232 (hardcover) |
ISBN 9780525560043 (international edition)
Subjects: LCSH: Time management. | Distraction
(Psychology) | Attention.
Classification: LCC BF637.T5 (ebook) | LCC BF637.T5 B349 2018
(print) | DDC 153.7/33—dc23
LC record available at https://lccn.loc.gov/2018023750

Printed in the United States of America
1 3 5 7 9 10 8 6 4 2

Set in Adobe Garamond Pro

DESIGNED BY MEIGHAN CAVANAUGH

For Ardyn

CONTENTS

PART ONE

HYPERFOCUS

PART TWO

SCATTERFOCUS

HYPERFOCUS

WHY FOCUS MATTERS

Attention Is Everywhere

'm writing these words over the sounds of clanging cutlery and muffled conversation at a small diner in Kingston, Ontario, Canada.

I've always been a fan of people-watching. There's so much to take in—how they dress, walk, converse, and act when they're either around or not around others. At a busy café, or at a diner like this, it's fun to see personalities collide like particles in an accelerator; to observe a guy's personality change when he switches from talking to his friend to chatting up the waitress; to watch the personalities of waitstaff shift when serving each table, adapting to large families, young couples.

In focusing on other people, I've made a lot of observations about what those people are *focusing on*. In any given moment, we are all focusing on *something*, even if we're just lost in our internal thoughts. Let's take a glance through the diner.

I turn my attention first to the two twentysomething girls at the table to my left, who are mostly focusing on their smartphones instead of each other. Between bouts of texting, they flip their phones facedown on the table. This, it seems, is a pretty pointless gesture—they've picked them back up thirty seconds later. While I can't make out their every word, I can tell they're skimming the surface of the conversation they could be having. They're with each other in person, but their attention is elsewhere.

Or take the couple across the room. They're engrossed in a conversation fueled by hot coffee and buttermilk pancakes. They were engaged in relatively quiet small talk when they arrived, but their conversation soon became more animated. Unlike the girls, this couple has focused only on each other since sitting down.

A catchy Ed Sheeran song comes on over the restaurant's speakers, and my attention is drawn to the two guys sitting a few tables over from the couple. One of them subtly taps his foot to the beat while his friend orders. The foot tapper is presumably spreading his attention across three things: the song, what his friend is ordering, and his own breakfast decision. After he orders the Three Egg Express, when the server asks how he'd like his eggs prepared, he directs his attention inward, seemingly recalling how he usually takes them. He orders scrambled.

At the bar are a few strangers making idle conversation while watching last night's football highlights. I find it especially fascinating that millions of people around the world, including these three guys, are fixated on an eleven-inch piece of tanned cowhide. As I watch, one of the guys cocks his head, lost in thought. Then, as though a shock wave was traveling through his body, he rushes to capture an idea in his pocketed notepad. While he was lost in a daydream, and to the tune of football highlights, an insight struck from out of the blue. He had a eureka moment.

Or take me, sitting here with my laptop. This morning, as I sip coffee and nibble home fries, I've been able to focus more deeply on my work and have more energy to burn. My morning meditation may have helped—I find I'm able to write more words when I take part in this ritual (40 percent more, by my calculations). I left my phone at home so I could write distraction free, and so my mind could rest on the walk to the diner, and wander. As I'll discuss later, disconnecting is one of the most powerful ways to spark new and innovative ideas. The music playing on the restaurant speakers is catchy, but not enough to be distracting. I'm not here for the soundtrack, though, and also chose this diner over my favorite café because there's no wi-fi—constant connectivity is one of the worst disruptions to our focus and productivity. As the last few paragraphs demonstrate, I am a bit distracted by the environment and the people it's hosting, but they're serving as good fodder for this introduction.

This restaurant scene is a handy illustration of a revelation I had awhile back: attention is all around us. Once you see it, you can't unsee it. Everyone awake on the planet, in this one moment—whether they're eating breakfast, working, or spending time with their family—is focused on something. Attention is the backdrop against which we live our lives wherever we go and whatever we do, even if we're just noticing the thoughts in our head.

It has been a few years since I first began to explore how we can not only focus better but also think more clearly. While this is tough to admit, especially as someone who was making his living as a "productivity expert," I started to notice my own increased distraction, especially as I accumulated more devices. I had never been so busy while accomplishing so little. I had grown restless with boredom and a lack of stimulation and was trying to cram as much into every moment as I could. I knew that my brain never functioned well when I was trying to multitask, but I felt compelled to do it anyway. Working with my email client open and my smartphone on my desk was simply more appealing than trying to concentrate on one or two simple things. For me, this book was born out of necessity: I wrote it because I needed it.

When I get excited by a new idea, I typically order dozens of books on it and nerd out about that topic. Focus has been my most recent fascination. This includes how we can best manage the distractions around us; multitask more effectively, if that's possible (it is); battle our resistance to focusing on tasks that make us procrastinate; and also better *un*focus so that we can genuinely relax and recharge. In my reading, I found an awful lot of information—advice (often contradictory) that was fun to read but ultimately didn't help me progress my work and life forward.

I then turned to the actual scientific research—scores of academic studies and decades of documentation dedicated to learning how we best focus.* As I carefully read every study I could find, the "Focus" folder on my computer became massive. I amassed tens of thousands of words of notes and began to identify the most practical, tactical lessons from them. I started speaking to the world's foremost attention researchers to get to the bottom of why we get distracted so easily and discover how we can get our stubborn minds to focus in a world of distraction. And I started to experiment with the research myself, to see if it was actually possible to get a grip on my focus.

What I discovered completely changed not only how I work but also how I live my life. I began to see focus as not only a contributor to my productivity but also a factor in my overall well-being. Surprisingly, I learned that one of the best practices for fostering my creativity and productivity was learning how to *un*focus. By paying attention to nothing in particular and letting my mind wander—as I did on my way to the Kingston diner—I found that I became better at making connections between ideas and coming up with new ones.

---

* Reading a research paper from front to back is *way* easier said than done—but pretty doable when you're interested in the topic. Curiously, research shows that what lets us focus when reading isn't the complexity of a paper or article—it's how *interested* we are in what we're reading.

I also found that we encounter more distraction today than we have in the entire history of humanity. Studies show we can work for an average of *just forty seconds* in front of a computer before we're either distracted or interrupted. (Needless to say, we do our best work when we attend to a task for a lot longer than forty seconds.) I went from viewing multitasking as a stimulating work hack to regarding it as a trap of continuous interruptions. While trying to do more tasks simultaneously, we prevent ourselves from finishing any one task of significance. And I began to discover that by focusing deeply on just one important thing at a time—hyperfocusing—we become the most productive version of ourselves.

Above all else I began to view attention as the most important ingredient we can add if we're to become more productive, creative, and happy—at work and at home. When we invest our limited attention intelligently and deliberately, we focus more deeply and think more clearly. This is an essential skill in today's world, when we are so often in distracting environments doing brain-heavy knowledge work.

This book takes you on a guided tour through my exploration of the subject of focus. I'll share not only the fascinating things I've learned but also how to actually put those ideas to use in your own life (I've road-tested all of them). Productivity research is great—but pretty useless when you don't act upon it. In this way, I see *Hyperfocus* as a sort of "science-help" book; one that explores the fascinating research behind how you focus but also bridges those insights with your daily life to explore ways you can manage your attention better to become more productive and creative. These ideas have already changed one life (mine), and I know they can do the same for you too. On the surface, the results can seem a bit like magic, but magic stops being magic the moment you know how it's done.

HOW TO BETTER FOCUS
ON THIS BOOK

Reading this book is your first chance to put your focus to the test, and the more attention you can dedicate to it, the more you'll get out of the time spent on it. Let's begin on a practical note with seven ways to focus more deeply while reading.

But first, a quick comment. If I've learned one thing from my research, it's that productivity is highly personal. Everyone is uniquely wired and has different routines—as a result, not all productivity tactics will mesh comfortably with your life. Not to mention the fact that you may simply not *want* to follow some of the advice I offer. Experiment with as many of these focus tactics as you can, and adopt whatever works for you.

1. PUT YOUR PHONE OUT OF SIGHT

When your mind is even *slightly* resisting a task, it will look for more novel things to focus on. Our smartphones are a great example—they provide an endless stream of bite-sized, delicious information for our brains to consume.

As I'll discuss later, distractions and interruptions are infinitely easier to deal with before they become a temptation. Start seeing your smartphone for what it really is: a productivity black hole that sits in your pocket. To focus on this book, I recommend leaving your device in another room. It may take your brain a few minutes to adjust to not having your phone or pad attached at your hip, but trust me, it's worth powering through that initial resistance. It's never healthy to be dependent on something—addictive, shiny rectangular devices included.

Here's a fun experiment to dive deeper into this idea: over the span of a day or two, pay attention to the number of times you instinctively pull out your phone. How are you feeling, and what compels you to reach for it? Are you trying to distract yourself during a long elevator ride? Are you avoiding a boring task, like updating your quarterly budget? By noting the times you habitually reach for your phone, you'll gain insight into which tasks you resist the most and how you're feeling in those moments.

2. MIND YOUR ENVIRONMENT

Look up and around you: Where are you reading this book? How likely are you to be distracted or interrupted as you read, and is there a place you could go to avoid those distractions? Or are you reading in an environment where you don't have much control, such as on the train or the subway?

Modifying your environment is one of the top ways to cultivate your focus. The most focus-conducive environments are those in which you're interrupted and distracted the least. If possible, move yourself to one of these places—whether it's a café down the street, the library, or a quieter room in the house.

3. MAKE A DISTRACTIONS LIST

Distractions will always be present, even if you manage to find a reading spot in a Japanese Zen garden with your phone far away. External distractions aren't the only ones to blame—think of the distractions that can come internally, like your brain reminding you that you need to pick up groceries.

Whenever I have to focus, I adopt the two tactics mentioned above—and I also bring a pen and a notepad with me. In the notepad I write every distraction that makes its way into my mind—things I need to follow up on, tasks I can't forget, new ideas, and so on.

Maintaining a distractions list as you read will capture the important things that float to the surface of your consciousness. Writing them down to make sure they don't slip through the cracks will let you refocus on the task at hand.

4. QUESTION WHETHER THIS BOOK IS WORTH CONSUMING AT ALL

We consume a lot of things out of habit, without questioning their worth—books included.

Take time to weigh the value of your routine consumption. A tactic I find helpful is to view the descriptions of books, TV shows, podcasts, and everything else as "pitches" for your time and attention. Ask yourself: After consuming one of those products, will you be happy with how you invested your time and attention?

Just as you are what you eat, you are what you pay attention to. Attention is finite and is the most valuable ingredient you have to live a good life—so make sure everything you consume is worthy of it. As I'll cover in depth later, bringing awareness to what you consume can provide *hours* of extra time each day.

5. CONSUME SOME CAFFEINE BEFORE READING

If it's not too late in the day—caffeine takes eight to fourteen hours to metabolize out of your system—consider reading alongside a cup of coffee or tea.

Caffeine provides an invaluable focus boost, and while you usually have to pay this energy back later in the day as the drug metabolizes out of your system, the costs are often worth it. Caffeine boosts your mental and physical performance in virtually every measurable way (more on page 207). Use this energy boost wisely to work on an important task or to read this book.

6. GRAB A PEN OR HIGHLIGHTER

There are two ways to consume information: passively and actively.

One of my (many) habits that bother my fiancée is that I tear out the first page of every book I read to use as a bookmark. (She argues this is sacrilegious; I say there are more copies of the same book at the store.) This is only the start of the carnage; I also read with a highlighter and a pen in hand so I can mark up the book as I read it. The number of highlights and notes on its pages indicates how much I liked it. When I finish that first read, I go through the book a second time, rereading just the highlighted parts so I can really process the most valuable nuggets. If I can, I'll annoy someone nearby by sharing these bits so I can process them again even more deeply.

I hope that while reading *Hyperfocus* you'll highlight and underline away, pulling the best ideas off its pages and carrying them in your mind to build and act upon later. If I've done a good job in writing it, you'll have made a large number of notes. (Please email me a picture of your finished work of art—I'd love to see it. My email, and other ways to contact me, are at the back of the book.)

7. WHEN YOU NOTICE YOUR FOCUS WAVERING . . .

Your ability to focus isn't limitless—while you can improve your attention span, it's only a matter of time until it begins to waver. This often takes the form of your mind wandering away from the words on the page to the thoughts in your head. This is perfectly normal and human—and, as we'll see later, this wandering can be remarkably powerful when harnessed.

For now, though, when you do notice your focus fading, step back from this book for a few minutes to do something relatively mindless. Whether it's washing the dishes, people watching, or cleaning the house, you'll effectively recharge your attention. Once your focus has been reset, return to the book with a fresh mind. And just as you've kept a distractions list while you read, make sure you have a place to capture ideas that come to mind during your break.

PART I

HYPERFOCUS

SWITCHING OFF AUTOPILOT MODE

AUTOPILOT MODE

Right now there's a good chance that you're focused on this book. But how did you get here?

Looking at the books in my own library, I learned about most of them through recommendations from friends, podcast appearances by the author, or having loved a similar book. Most of us don't deliberately plot out which element of our lives we want to improve before settling on a book that will help us address that issue. We often arrive at those reading decisions because of a confluence of events.

Take, for example, the last book I read. One day I was riding in a taxi whose driver had the radio on, and I heard an interview with the author. Later, a friend tweeted about that book twice. This accumulation of mentions led to my eventual decision to buy the book. The process as a whole was anything but deliberate.

Our not plotting out in detail everything we do and every decision we make is, for the most part, a good thing. I made the series of decisions involved in purchasing many of my books in autopilot mode. Autopilot mode enables us to keep up with the demands of our life. For example, imagine if every email response required you to draft your answer in a new Word document. From there, you'd have to reread it several times, send it to your significant other for improvements, and print it once or twice to do line edits, only to arrive several hours later at a final, eloquent "Sure, sounds good!" This might be a productive thing to do for an important project, but for every email? Imagine being just as deliberate buying ketchup, taking out the trash, or brushing your teeth.

Autopilot mode guides us through actions like these. As many as 40 percent of our actions are habits, which shouldn't require conscious deliberation. Unless you're a monk and have the luxury of being able to meditate all day, it's impossible to live intentionally 100 percent of the time.

But some decisions *are* worth making deliberately. How we manage our attention is one of them.

We typically manage our attention on autopilot. When we receive an email from our boss, we instinctively stop what we're doing to respond to it. When someone has posted a picture of us online, we check to see how we look, then click to read what the poster said about us. When we're talking with a coworker or a loved one, we automatically focus on forming clever responses in our head before she finishes her thought. (One of the most underrated skills: letting other people finish their sentences before starting yours.)

Here's a simple exercise that'll take you thirty seconds. Come up with an honest answer to this question: throughout the day, how frequently do you *choose* what to focus on? In other words, roughly how much of your time do you spend deliberately and with intention, deciding in advance what you want to do and when you'll do it?

Most people don't fare too well with their answers. We lead busy lives, and at most we only occasionally choose to focus on something intentionally—when we catch ourselves daydreaming, sense that we've been procrastinating, fall into the trap of bouncing around the same several apps or websites, or realize we've zoned out while watching our kids.

After we snap out of autopilot mode, we consider what we really ought to be doing and make the effort to realign our neurons to focus on that instead.

While falling into autopilot mode can help us keep up the pace of work and life, attention is our most limited and constrained resource. The more we can manage our attention with intention, the more focused, productive, and creative we become.

A DAY IN AUTOPILOT MODE

The environments in which we live and work, unfortunately, have their own agenda for claiming our attention, bombarding us with alerts, notifications, beeps, and buzzes. This steady stream of interruptions prevents us from diving into any one thing properly; after all, it isn't long before we're presented with another email that feels just as urgent.

If you're still here, you're probably better at focusing than the average person. Reading a book requires a good deal of attention—and with attention becoming a rare commodity, fewer people are able to devote themselves to reading without distraction. But it's worth quickly asking: How much of your attention are you directing to this paragraph in this moment? Are you focused on it 100 percent? 85 percent? 50 percent? How has your level of focus changed over time, especially as you moved from one environment to another? How frequently has your mind wandered from the words on this page to the thoughts in your head—eyes skimming focus free until you caught yourself and tuned back in?* Even the most experienced, focused readers have these mind-wandering episodes.

It's not unusual to have a hard time focusing. There are countless everyday examples of how little control we have over our attention in our daily lives. Take, for example the following:

- How our mind refuses to shut off when we're lying in bed at night. While a large part of us wants to sleep because we have things to do in the morning, our mind insists on reliving the entire day.
- How our mind brings up cringeworthy memories at the worst possible times. Where do these thoughts come from?
- How incredible ideas and insights come to us while our mind is wandering in the shower, but the same insights don't strike when we need them the most.
- How we find ourselves having forgotten our reason for entering the kitchen or bedroom. Why did we lose our grip on our original intention?
- How we can't focus on something when we want to—like writing a report that's not on a deadline. Or why we procrastinate and focus on things that aren't productive instead of spending our time productively.
- How we find ourselves in bed bouncing around a loop of the same five smartphone apps, checking for updates again and again until we snap out of our trance. We may fall into a similar

---

* Curiously, research shows that our eyes actually scan the page *more slowly* when our mind is wandering—our eyes and our mind are "tightly coupled." Becoming aware of when your scanning begins to slow will help you halt these mind-wandering episodes with greater ease. Future developments in technology could lead to tablets and e-readers that catch our mind-wandering episodes before we do.

mindless loop on the internet—switching between news websites, IM conversations, and social media.

- How we're unable to stop worrying about certain things until
  they're resolved or vanish into the ether.

As you read *Hyperfocus* and learn to focus more deliberately, these
lapses will make a lot more sense, and you'll even learn how to prevent them.

THE FOUR TYPES OF TASKS

In many ways, managing your attention is like choosing what to watch
on Netflix. When you first launch the website, you're presented with a
landing page highlighting just a few of the many shows that are available. The Netflix homepage is like a fork in the road—only instead of
two paths forward, there are thousands. Taking some of those paths
will leave you feeling happy, some will mindlessly entertain you, and
others will teach you something useful.

Deciding where to direct our attention presents a similar fork in the
road—only the pathways lead to the innumerable things on which we
can choose to focus. Right now you're absorbed in this book. But if you
look up from this page or your e-reader, you'll see many alternative
objects of attention. Some are more meaningful and productive than
others. Focusing on this book is probably more productive than focusing on your smartphone, the wall, or the music in the background. If
you're grabbing breakfast with a friend, focusing on him or her is infinitely more rewarding than watching the football highlights playing in
the background.

When you tally up all of the potential things on which you could
focus in your external environment, there is truly an overwhelming

number of options. And that's not even counting the trivia, ideas, and memories in your own head.

This is the problem with managing your attention on autopilot mode. The most urgent and stimulating things in your environment are rarely the most significant. This is why switching off autopilot mode is so critical. **Directing your attention toward the most important object of your choosing—and then sustaining that attention—is the most consequential decision we will make throughout the day. We are what we pay attention to.**

To make sense of all of the things bidding for our focus, it's helpful to divide our tasks into categories. I'll discuss focus here largely as it pertains to work, but these rules apply just as much to your life at home, as several sections later in the book will explore.

There are two main criteria to consider when categorizing what to focus on: whether a task is productive (you accomplish a lot by doing it) and whether a task is attractive (fun to do) or unattractive (boring, frustrating, difficult, etc.).

FOUR TYPES OF TASKS

	UNATTRACTIVE	ATTRACTIVE
PRODUCTIVE	Necessary Work	Purposeful Work
UNPRODUCTIVE	Unnecessary Work	Distracting Work

I'll refer to this grid quite often, so let's quickly take a look at each of the four categories of tasks.

Necessary work includes tasks that are unattractive yet productive. Team meetings and calls about your quarterly budget fall into this quadrant. We usually have to push ourselves to do this type of work.

Unnecessary work includes the tasks that are both unproductive and unattractive—like rearranging the papers on your desk or the files on your computer. We usually don't bother with these tasks unless we're procrastinating on doing something else or resisting a task that falls into the necessary work or purposeful work categories. Spending time on unnecessary work tasks keeps us busy, but such busyness is just an active form of laziness when it doesn't lead to actually accomplishing anything.

Distracting work includes stimulating, unproductive tasks and as such is a black hole for productivity. It includes social media, most IM conversations, news websites, watercooler chats, and every other form of low-return distraction. These activities can be fun but should generally be indulged in small doses. The better you become at managing your attention, the less time you'll spend in this quadrant.

The remaining box on the chart is **purposeful work**—the productivity sweet spot. These are the tasks we're put on earth to do; the tasks we're most engaged in as we do them; the tasks with which we make the largest impact. Very few tasks fit into this box—most people I've encountered have three or four at most. Doing good work in this category usually requires more brainpower, and we are often better at these types of tasks than other people are. An actor's most purposeful tasks might be to rehearse and perform. A financial adviser's purposeful tasks might be to make investments, meet with clients, and educate herself on industry trends. A researcher's most important tasks might include designing and running studies, teaching, and applying for funding. My most important tasks are writing books and blog articles, reading research to encounter new ideas, and giving talks. In your personal life, your purposeful tasks might include spending time with your kids, working on a side hustle, or volunteering with a local charity.

A perfectly productive person would focus on only the top two quadrants of the above chart. If things were that simple, though, you wouldn't need this book. As you've no doubt experienced, sticking within the borders of necessary and purposeful work is much easier said than done. Every day, tasks from all four quadrants compete for our attention. Working on autopilot means we are more prone to falling prey to the unnecessary and distracting ones and often spend time on necessary and purposeful work only when we're on deadline.

I noticed something interesting as I applied the research in this book to my own life: as time passed, I began to spend less time on autopilot and focused more attention on my most purposeful and necessary tasks. As you become more deliberate about managing your attention, I think you'll find the same to be true for your work.

> Here's an immediate way to improve your productivity. Divide up your work tasks based on the four categories in the above grid. This simple activity will give you an incredible awareness of what's actually important in your work. Because I'll return to the grid often going forward, divvying up your work activities will be valuable as you make your way through the book.

CHAPTER 2

THE LIMITS OF YOUR ATTENTION

Without selective interest, experience is utter chaos.

—*William James*

Your focus determines your reality.

—*Qui-Gon Jinn, Star Wars: Episode I: The Phantom Menace*

THE BOUNDARIES OF YOUR ATTENTION

Our attention is the most powerful tool we have to live a good life and get stuff done, but our ability to focus is constrained in two main ways.

First, **there's a finite limit to how many things we can focus on.** That limit is smaller than you might think. If we could actually focus on more tasks simultaneously, we'd be able to do far more in the moment: memorizing someone's phone number while playing the piano, carrying on a conversation with two people, and responding to an email on our phone. Realistically we can, at most, do one or two of these things well at the same time.

Our environment sends a steady stream of information to our brain every second. Think about the sights, sounds, and other information coming at you in this moment, and you'll realize there is a nearly infinite number of items at which you could direct your focus. Timothy

Wilson, a professor of psychology at the University of Virginia, esti-
mates that our brain receives eleven million "bits" of information in
the form of sensory experiences each second.

But how many of these eleven million bits can our minds consciously process and focus on at once? Just *forty* of them. Not forty
million or forty *thousand*, but forty.

When we choose what to focus on, we're effectively sipping from a
fire hose. One conversation, for example, consumes the majority of our
attentional bits, which is why we can't carry on two at once. According
to renowned psychologist Mihaly Csikszentmihalyi, simply *decoding* a
conversation (so we can understand it) consumes more than half of our
attention. As well as interpreting a person's words, you have to parse
the meaning behind what he or she is saying. While you're conversing,
there are countless other places to direct your remaining attentional
bits: your work tasks for tomorrow, random thoughts in your head, the
lamp behind your partner, the timbre of her voice, or what you're going
to say next—but extracting the meaning of what you're hearing is the
best use of your focus.

The second way that our attention is limited is that **after focusing
on something, we can hold only a small amount of information in
our short-term memory.** The ability to temporarily store information
in our minds is practically a superpower, as it's what enables us to think
about what we're doing as we're doing it, whether that involves problem-
solving tasks (e.g., carrying over digits when doing arithmetic) or planning for the future (e.g., plotting the best sequence of exercises at the
gym). Without this temporary mental scratch pad, we'd be mindlessly
reacting to whatever was happening in the world around us.

When it comes to holding information in our temporary memory,
though, the magic number of which our brain is capable shrinks from
forty to *four*. Try to memorize the following list of names and then
write them down:

- Ardyn
- Rick
- Ryan
- Lucinda
- Luise
- Martin
- Kelsea
- Sinisa
- Dwight
- Bryce

When asked to write the names they remember, some people are able to recall only three, while others can manage five, six, or even seven. The average number, though, is four.

In this context the number four refers to unique *chunks* of information. For example, if you can find a way to connect a few of the names into such chunks— such as visualizing a few friends who have the same names as the ones on the list—you'll be able to process them more deeply and remember more. In my case, I can remember all ten names and still have room to spare. I'm not some supergenius, though—to create the list I picked the names of the ten people I emailed the most this week, which enabled me to effortlessly group them together for memory's sake.

We can use this concept of "chunking" things together to better remember any number of practical things throughout the day. This morning I was listening to an audiobook while getting groceries—a difficult combination to do simultaneously. I needed to buy three things: celery, hummus, and crackers. When I walked into the store, I visualized a triangle with the location of each of the three items as one of its points. Instead of struggling to remember my grocery list independently, I was able to walk the triangle. Visualizing a meal consisting of the same three ingredients would have done the trick too and is probably an even simpler idea.

Our lives are generally structured around the fact that we're able to hold, at most, seven pieces of unique information in our short-term memory. You need look no further than the world around you to see evidence of how we organize data into mentally orderly units. Start with the number two—there are countless examples in pop culture that show the power of the pair. We can easily hold two things in memory at once, so it's no accident that combinations of two are found everywhere, from dynamic duos like Batman and Robin to Bert and Ernie to Calvin and Hobbes. The number three also fits comfortably in our attentional space: we award three Olympic medals and grow up with stories like "Goldilocks and the Three Bears," "The Three Blind Mice," and "The Three Little Pigs." The list goes on: we divide these stories into three parts (the beginning, middle, and end) and have sayings like "Good things come in threes," "Celebrities die in threes," and "Third time's the charm." We also group ideas into fours (the four seasons), fives (the five "love languages"), sixes (the six sides of a die), and sevens (days of the week, deadly sins, and Wonders of the World). Even most phone numbers fit comfortably within this attentional limit: one set of three numbers (or maybe four, if you're in the United Kingdom), followed by another four digits, making the full number easy to hold in your mind as you dial. You have to dig deep to find common examples of groups larger than seven.

MEET YOUR ATTENTIONAL SPACE

"Attentional space" is the term I use to describe the amount of mental capacity we have available to focus on and process things in the moment. Our attentional space is what we're aware of at any given time—it's the scratch pad or clipboard in our brain that we use to temporarily store information as it's being processed. Attentional space allows us to hold, manipulate, and connect information simultaneously, and on the fly. When we choose what to pay attention to, that information occupies our short-term memory, and our attentional space ensures it's kept active so we can continue to work with it. Together, our focus and attentional space are responsible for most of our conscious experiences. If your brain were a computer, your attentional space would be its RAM. (Technically speaking, researchers refer to this space as our "working memory" and the size of this space as our "working memory capacity.")*

We'll discuss attentional space in considerable depth in *Hyperfocus*. Given that this space is so small and can hold only a few things at once, it's essential we manage it well. Even when we're daydreaming and focusing on nothing in particular, we fill our attentional space. When we focus on a conversation we're having, that conversation claims our complete attentional space (at least when it's interesting). Streaming a video while cooking dinner crams both these tasks into our attentional space. When we retrieve a memory or fact (like a friend's birthday or the name of a song) from our long-term memory, this information is temporarily loaded into our attentional space for when we need it.

---

* A computer or phone with more RAM can run faster because it can hold more in memory. Higher RAM invariably compromises your battery life, though—especially on a phone. Apple recently resisted adding more RAM to its iPhone for this reason. Since the RAM on a computer is always active, and information is constantly moving through it, that activity sucks up a lot of power. Our attentional space may be limited for a similar reason. Some scientists argue that it might have been "biologically expensive" for us to have evolved to have a larger attentional space, because of how activated our brain would need to be—and how much energy it would need to consume—to keep that information simultaneously activated. In addition, over the last 2.5 million years, our daily tasks weren't nearly as complex as the knowledge work we do today. Our brain consumes enough energy as it is. While it makes up just 2–3 percent of our body mass, it burns 20 percent of the calories we take in. The fact that our brain's capacity is limited in this way allows us to conserve energy, which may have aided our chances at survival.

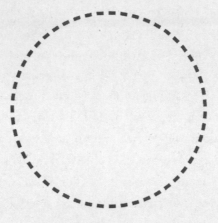

ATTENTIONAL SPACE

The space holds everything that you're aware of—it's your entire conscious world.

I find reading—and the science that studies how it fills attentional space—a particularly fascinating subject. If you're truly paying attention to the words on this page, you have almost no attentional space remaining for other tasks. Just as you don't have sufficient attentional space to both text and drive, you can't text while you read—either of these two tasks alone requires too much focus to fit comfortably in your attentional space. At best, you might be able to drink a cup of coffee while reading, but there's a chance it could get cold if you become too immersed in the text—or you might spill some on the book when you try, and fail, to do both.

As you read, your brain is hard at work converting the raw bits of perceptual information into facts, stories, and lessons that you remember and internalize. After your eyes register the waves of light emanating from the page, your mind generates words from them. These words temporarily fill your attentional space. You then begin connecting the words to form syntactic units and clauses—the fundamental building blocks of sentences. Finally, using your attentional space as a scratch pad, your brain groups *those* combinations of words together into complete ideas so you can extract their higher-level meaning.

Sentence structure can influence this process and slow down or speed up how quickly you read. Much as the world doesn't combine many groups of data into sets greater than seven, every book is structured to accommodate a reader's restricted attentional space. Sentences have a limited length and are punctuated by commas, semicolons, and dashes. According to one study, the period at the end of a sentence is the point when our attentional space "stops being loaded, and what has been present in it up to that moment, must be in some way stored in a summarized form in a short-term memory."

Your attention is constantly synced to what you're reading or doing. Here's an interesting example: you even *blink* in accordance with where your attention is directed. You normally blink fifteen to twenty times a minute but do so during natural breaks in your attention—such as at the end of a sentence when reading, when someone you're speaking with pauses, or at breakpoints when watching a video. This blinking rhythm happens automatically—all you have to do is pay attention to what you're reading, and your brain's attentional space takes care of the rest.

WHAT'S FILLING YOUR ATTENTIONAL SPACE?

Let's do a quick check-in. What's occupying your attentional space at this moment? In other words, what's on your mind?

Are this book and your thoughts about it consuming 100 percent of your attentional space? If so, you'll process it faster and better. Are you devoting a third of your attention to thinking about the smartphone by your side? Is part of your mind planning what you'll do after completing this chapter or distracted by something you're worried about? Are these concerns or anxieties popping out of nowhere?

Directing your mental gaze to what is currently occupying your attentional space can be an odd exercise, as we rarely notice what has taken hold of our attention but spend most of our time totally immersed in what we're experiencing. There's a term for this process: meta-awareness. Becoming aware of what you're thinking about is one of the best practices for managing your attention. The more you notice what's occupying your attentional space, the faster you can get back on track when your mind begins to wander, which it does a remarkable *47 percent* of the time.

Whether you're writing an email, taking part in a conference call, watching a TV show, or having dinner with your family, you're essentially spending half of your time and attention on what's *not* in front of you, lost in the past or calculating the future. That's a lot of time and attention to waste. While there is immense value in letting your mind scatter, most times we'd do better to focus on the present.

This is essentially what mindfulness is—noticing what your *mind* is *full* of: what you're thinking, feeling, and perceiving at any given moment. Mindfulness adds another important dimension to the mix: not judging what you're thinking about. When you become aware of what is occupying your mind, you realize it can come up with some pretty crazy stuff, not all of which is true—like the negative self-talk that sometimes takes root in your head. Everyone's mind does this on some level, so you shouldn't sweat it too much or take all of your thoughts too seriously. As one of my favorite writers, David Cain, puts it, "All thoughts want to be taken seriously, but few warrant it."

Simply *noticing* what is occupying our attentional space has been shown to make us more productive. One study asked participants to read a detective novel and try to solve the crime. It compared readers whose minds wandered *without* awareness with those whose minds wandered *consciously*. Solve rates were substantially higher for the group that was aware that their minds had wandered. We perform significantly better on every task when we're aware that our mind is wandering.

If you pay attention to what's on your mind—which is admittedly hard to do for more than a minute or so—you'll notice that the content of your attentional space is constantly changing. You'll understand that it truly *is* a scratch pad, with thoughts, tasks, conversations, projects, daydreams, conference calls, and other objects of attention continually passing through. You'll also find that your attentional space expands and shrinks depending on your mood. Objects of attention fade from this space just as quickly as they came—usually without your awareness. For all the power it provides, the content of your attentional space is ephemeral; its memory lasts for an average of just ten seconds.

TASKS THAT PAIR WELL

So what exactly can fit comfortably within attentional space?

Tasks take different amounts of attentional space depending on their complexity. A meaningful conversation (as opposed to a casual one) fills up most, if not all, of it. That conversation will suffer as a result of trying to cram too many other things into your attentional space. When you leave your phone on the table during a conversation, for example, you're bound to be distracted by the possibility of incoming messages.

Not all tasks require this much attentional space. There are two kinds of tasks in our life and work: habits, which we can perform without much thought and require minimal attentional space, and complex tasks, which can be done well only with dedicated focus. Many experts argue that we can't multitask, which is often true for tasks that require focus to do properly and thus occupy a larger amount of attentional space. But the same is not true for habits—in fact, we're able to multitask *surprisingly well* with habits. Though we may not be able to carry on two conversations simultaneously, we can walk, breathe, and chew bubblegum while we listen to an audiobook—the last task being one that will easily occupy what's left of our attention.

Habitual tasks like cutting your nails, doing the laundry, archiving emails you've already read, and grocery shopping don't require nearly as much attention as more complex tasks. This makes it possible to multitask without compromising the quality of your actions. Every Sunday I like to lump my personal, relatively rote "maintenance tasks" together—tasks that help me maintain who I am, like preparing meals, trimming my nails, and cleaning the house—and do them all in an allotted period of time while listening to podcasts or an audiobook. It's easily one of my favorite weekly rituals. You can do the same, for example, on your daily commute: if you listen to an audiobook during that routine, hourlong trip, you'll be able to read an extra book each week by utilizing the attention freed by a habitual task.

Habits take up very little attentional space, because they take little thought once we get going with them. As cognitive neuroscientist Stanislas Dehaene, author of *Consciousness and the Brain*, told me, "If you think of habits such as playing the piano, dressing, shaving, or driving on a familiar route, these are so automatic that they do not seem to prevent any conscious thought." He says that while habits like these may require some level of conscious *initiation*, once we begin the behavior, the rest of the process takes care of itself. We may need to make conscious decisions occasionally—such as when we're getting dressed and our usual Tuesday outfit is in the wash—but after that intervention we can switch back to the rest of the habit sequence without much thought. Dehaene believes that this process is "presumably driven by sequence-related activity" in the brain. The brain even assists when we try to do more than one habitual thing simultaneously, by rerouting blood flow away from the prefrontal cortex—the brain's logic center—to the basal ganglia, which helps us run through the habitual sequences of daily routines.

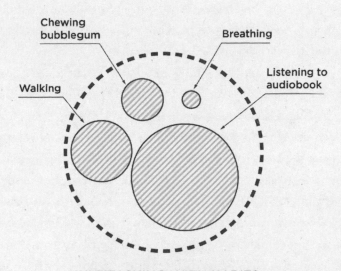

MULTITASKING WITH HABITS

Our attentional space can process even more when we're working on unrelated tasks. Take sorting and putting away the laundry while talking on the phone, for example. These activities tap into several senses— sorting laundry into our motor and visual senses; the phone call into our auditory sense. Because we use different brain regions to process them, the tasks aren't competing for the same mental resources. There is a tipping point to attentional space, of course—doing too many habitual tasks at the same time will cause your attentional space to become overloaded. This is especially true if what you're doing isn't totally automatic and requires frequent mental intervention. Ultimately the point is this: the number of habitual tasks we can fit into our attentional space is much higher than the number of demanding ones.

Tasks that we *can't* do out of habit—such as reading a book, having a deep conversation, or preparing a progress report for our boss—consume significantly more attentional space, because doing them well demands that we consciously manipulate information on the fly. If we tried carrying on a conversation with our significant other out of habit, we'd probably not process or remember it and find ourselves falling back on statements like "Yes, dear."

If you divided your work tasks into the four categories I described in chapter 1 (page 20)—an activity I highly recommend because I'll be referencing it later—you'll notice that your most necessary and pur-poseful tasks can't be done out of habit.* This is exactly what makes these tasks so productive. You accomplish more in doing them because they require focus and brainpower and take advantage of unique skill sets. Anyone can do mindless work out of habit. This is one of the many reasons why distracting tasks are so costly: while these tasks are attractive and stimulating (think watching Netflix after a long day at the office instead of grabbing dinner with a friend), they steal precious time from your most productive work.

Spending time on our most productive tasks means we usually have very little attention to spare—if there's any left at all.

Unlike habitual tasks, we aren't able to fit two complex activities into our attentional space at the same time. Remember, we can focus only on forty bits of information, and a single complex task requires most of these bits—and on top of this limit, we can process only so much at one time.

---

* If you *can* do your most productive tasks out of habit, it's a sign you should probably delegate them to someone else, eliminate them entirely, or make a conscious effort to spend less time and attention on them.

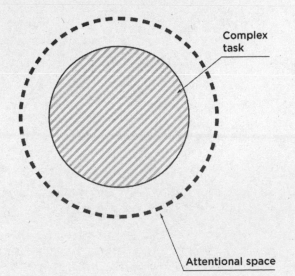

Complex
task

Attentional space

Since even moderately complex tasks consume most of our attention, we're *at best* able to pair something habitual with a more complex task.

There is no easy way to predict how much attentional space a task will consume—for example, driving will demand much less if you're an expert than if you're a driver's ed student. You're better able to chunk together information on the fly when you have experience with a given

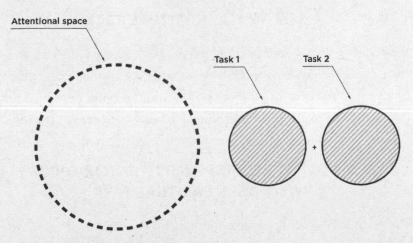

Attentional space

Task 1   Task 2

WHEN MULTITASKING DOESN'T WORK

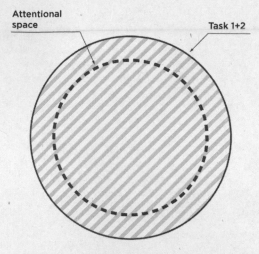

WHEN MULTITASKING DOESN'T WORK

task, which provides more freedom to focus on other things. Another variable is the actual size of your attentional space—a measure that's different for everyone.

In summary, there are generally three combinations of tasks that fit comfortably within your attentional space.

1. A FEW SMALL, HABITUAL TASKS

We're able to breathe while we run, pay attention to our heart rate, and enjoy music—all at the same time. As mentioned earlier, initiating these habits requires attention, and then another attention boost if we need to intervene to stay on track (or, if we're listening to music, to *change* the track).

2. A TASK THAT REQUIRES MOST OF OUR FOCUS, AS WELL AS A HABITUAL TASK

Our attentional space is powerful but it's also very limited. At best, we can do one small, habitual task *plus* one other activity that requires most of our attention. Two examples: listening to a podcast or audio-book while doing maintenance tasks, or playing a simple, repetitive video game on a phone while listening to an audiobook.

Filling the rest of your attentional space with habitual, mindless tasks is often not the best way to use spare attention, so when possible, avoid loading it to the brim.

3. ONE COMPLEX TASK

Your most productive tasks—the ones that enable you to accomplish significantly more for every minute you dedicate to them—fall into this category. The more time and attention you spend on these tasks, the more productive you become.

The amount of attentional space consumed by complex tasks varies over time. While carrying on a discussion with your boss, for example, your attentional space may shrink and expand rhythmically to match the content of the conversation, allowing your mind both to wander and to focus on the conversation when it becomes more complex. In a team meeting you could, in an instant, go from being a passive ob-server to getting called on for a progress update.

Having some attentional space to spare during complex tasks allows you to do two things:

It leaves room to reflect on the best approach to completing the task, so you can work smarter and avoid autopilot mode. You'll be able to come up with ideas you might not have had if you were filling your attention to the brim—such as the realization that you could scrap the introduction of the presentation you're going to give and instead dive directly to the point.

Leaving some space also enables you to work with a greater aware-ness of where you should be directing your attention in the first place. That means you can better refocus when your mind inevitably wanders from the task at hand. At the same time, you have attentional space to spare if the task suddenly becomes even more complex.

ATTENTION OVERLOAD

Fitting the right amount and type of tasks into attentional space is both an art and an investment in productivity. The costs of overloading our attention can be pretty severe.

Have you ever walked into your kitchen or living room and realized you've forgotten why you went there in the first place? You've fallen into an attention overload trap. You tried to cram too many things into your attentional space—the TV show that was playing in the background, random thoughts, and the IMDb page you just read—and didn't have enough space left for your original intention. In this case, you meant to grab the grocery list your partner left on the dining room table.

The same thing happens when work problems weigh on your mind as you drive home from the office. In this situation, your mind may be even more full: decoding and processing the talk show on the radio while ruminating on what happened at work that day while running through the multiple habit sequences that let you drive home largely on autopilot mode. If you had planned on buying bread on the way, chances are you won't have enough space to accommodate even that small, simple intention. You'll arrive home feeling overwhelmed, and only in the morning will you open the bread drawer and remember the previous day's task.

We have to work with intention as much as possible—this is especially true when we have more to do than time within which to do it. Intention enables us to prioritize so we don't overload our attentional space. Doing so also leaves us feeling more calm: just as you likely feel uncomfortable after overeating, stuffing your attentional space with too many tasks can make you feel unsettled.

At any one time, your attentional space should hold at most two key things that you are processing: what you intend to accomplish and what you're currently doing. This isn't possible 100 percent of the time, especially as you become immersed in a task, but by being mindful of your intention, you can be confident that what you're immersed in is what you're actually aiming to get done.

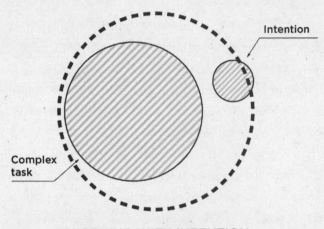

Intention

Complex task

WORKING WITH INTENTION

If you find yourself responding to important work in autopilot mode, chances are you're trying to cram too much into your attentional space. By not stepping back to deliberately manage your attention, you allow it to overflow. Some familiar examples:

- Taking care of your toddler while shopping.
- Trying to walk and text at the same time. Just this morning I watched someone bump into a mailbox because they were trying to do this.

- Rewinding a movie, TV show, or audiobook because someone was talking to you or because you simply zoned out for a while.
- Adding baking soda instead of baking powder to a recipe, because you were ruminating on something or watching TV.
- Leaving a theater with a stomachache, because you didn't have enough attention left to notice you'd eaten too much popcorn.
- Forgetting to put the divider on the grocery store checkout belt for the next person, like the lady in front of me forgot to do this morning as she flipped through a magazine.

You've probably experienced many similar moments. Some are impossible to avoid, because life often presents us with unexpected surprises. But many *are* possible to circumvent, and noticing that you're beginning to feel overwhelmed is a great sign that you should check in to assess what's occupying your attentional space. Chances are you're trying to cram too much into it at once.

The best way to avoid this overload is to be more selective with what you permit into your attentional space. On the drive home, shut off the radio, which will enable you to process the day and also remember your intention to pick up bread. At home, pause or mute the TV so you don't try to continue processing the show and forget that you're heading to fetch a note that's in the other room. Making small changes like these allows you to keep your attention on your intention.

Simplifying our attentional space lets us maintain enough room to work and live intentionally throughout the day. This lets us spend more time on what's important and meaningful in the moment. The state of your attentional space determines the state of your life. When your attentional space is overwhelmed, you, in turn, feel overwhelmed. When your attentional space is clear, you also feel clear. The tidier you keep your attentional space, the more clearly you think.

Time for a quick check-in: what's occupying your attentional space at this moment? Take stock of everything that's on your mind. If you find that your attentional space is a bit too full, simplify what's in it, either by writing down these things so you can deal with them later or by refocusing on the book in your hands.

Simplifying what we focus on in the moment may feel counterintuitive: when we have so much to get done, our natural impulse is to focus on as much as possible. Compounding this is the fact that the brain's prefrontal cortex—the large part of the forebrain that lets us plan, think logically, and get work done—has a built-in "novelty bias." Whenever we switch between tasks, it rewards us with dopamine—that amazing pleasure chemical that rushes through our brain whenever we devour a medium-sized pizza, accomplish something awesome, or have a drink or two after work. You may have noticed that you instinctively reach for your tablet when you sit down to watch TV, that you can't resist keeping your email open in another window as you work, or that you feel more stimulated when your phone is by your side. Continually seeking novel stimuli makes us *feel* more productive—after all, we're doing more in each moment. But again, just because we're busier doesn't mean we're getting more accomplished.

Almost every book in the wellness space has an obligatory section discussing how the brain is primitive, and that we have to learn to rise above the impulses it gives rise to. This book is no exception. An unfortunate truth is that the brain is not built to do knowledge work—it's wired for survival and reproduction. We have evolved to crave things that provide us with a surge of dopamine, which reinforces habits and behaviors that have historically aided our chances at survival. Our brain provides a hit of dopamine after sex as a reward for procreating. It does so when we consume sugar, which is energy-dense and enables us to survive longer with less food, which was useful early in our evolution, when conditions weren't as bountiful as they are today.

Our brains also reward us for poorly managing our attention, because for our early ancestors, seeking novel threats in the environment aided their chance of survival. Instead of focusing so deeply on stoking a fire that they were not alert to a prowling tiger, early humans were constantly scanning for potential dangers around them. If that made them a bit less efficient in attending to the fire, they survived to see another day (and start another fire!).

Today the only nearby tigers are at the zoo, and the novelty bias that once benefited us now works actively against us. The devices we own—our TV, tablet, computer, and smartphone included—are infinitely more stimulating than the other productive and meaningful things we could be focusing on, and so with fewer predators to worry about, we naturally focus on our electronics instead.

After years of researching the topic, I've found that "productivity" has become a bit of a loaded term. What it usually connotes is a condition that feels cold, corporate, and overly focused on efficiency. I prefer a different (and friendlier) definition: productivity means accomplishing what we intend to. If our plan today is to write three thousand words, rock a presentation with our leadership team, and catch up on our email, and we successfully accomplish all of those, we were perfectly productive. Likewise, if we intend to have a relaxing day and manage to do absolutely nothing, we're again perfectly productive. Being *busy* doesn't make us productive. It doesn't matter how busy we are if that busyness doesn't lead us to accomplish anything of importance. Productivity is not about cramming more into our days but about doing *the right thing* in each moment.

THE COSTS ADD UP

It bears repeating that **there is nothing inherently wrong with multi-tasking.** It's entirely possible to multitask, especially when it comes to the habitual tasks in our work and life. But it's important to make a distinction between shifting our attention and multitasking. Multitasking means concurrently trying to focus on more than one thing at a time. Shifting our attention is the movement of our attentional spotlight (or our attentional space) from one task to another. Shifting attention throughout the day is necessary; if we focused on just one thing all day long, no matter how important it was, we probably wouldn't have a job. Still, too much shifting can be dangerous, especially when we're surrounded by more novel objects and distractions than our brain is capable of handling.

While slipping into autopilot mode is the largest cost of attention overflow, there are other disadvantages as well. For starters, letting your attentional space overflow affects your memory. You may have noticed that when you watch TV or a movie with your phone by your side, you recall much less of what you've seen. In fact, I've noticed that as I've allowed more devices into my life, I remember less in general. Technology speeds up time by tempting us in each moment to fill our attention to the brim. This leads us to remember less, because it is only when we pay attention to something that our brain actively encodes it into memory.*

When we make our attentional space juggle too many tasks, we fail to notice and remember the details of our most important work. When we multitask, we even process our work with *an entirely different part of*

---

* This is why you should deliberately pay more attention to tasks you recently forgot— shutting off the oven, for example. Studying works for the same reason: by paying attention to information multiple times, you are more likely to remember it.

our brain. Take studying as an example. As Russell Poldrack, a psychology professor at Stanford, explained to me, "When we learn while we multitask, we rely more heavily on the basal ganglia, a brain system that's involved in the learning of skills and habits." However, "when we encode information in a more focused state, we rely more heavily on our brain's hippocampus—which actually lets us store and recall the information."

What use is our time if not to create memories—of conversations, meals, vacations, and other experiences? When we fail to focus deeply on any one thing, we focus instead only on the "highlights" of what we're doing and, as a consequence, later forget how we spent our time. Letting our attention overflow makes our actions less meaningful, because we don't remember how we spent our time in the first place. This affects our productivity in the long run: we make more mistakes because we don't properly encode the lessons we learned the first time we messed up. We also accumulate less knowledge, which, when we do knowledge work for a living, sets us back in the long run.

Constantly shifting our attentional spotlight to focus on one thing and then another and then another not only prevents the formation of memories but also undermines our productivity. Research shows that the more often we fill our attention to the brim, the longer it takes us to switch between tasks, the less we're able to filter out irrelevant information on the fly, and the poorer we become at suppressing the urge to switch between tasks in the first place.

As I mentioned back in chapter 0, when we're working in front of a computer—a device that's obviously chock full of novel things to focus

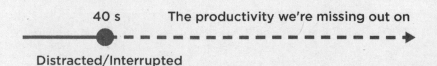

40 s   The productivity we're missing out on

Distracted/Interrupted

on—on average, we work for just *forty seconds* before we're either interrupted or distracted (or in other words, interrupt ourselves). This number becomes even more concerning when you consider the fact that our phone is by our side and interrupting us as well. Needless to say, our best work happens beyond this forty-second mark—nearly every single important task takes more than forty seconds of focused attention to do well.*

On top of the obvious productivity toll of continually interrupting ourselves, we're also not that good at shifting our attention. Even when our attentional space is relatively clear and focused on just one task, there are deep costs associated with switching quickly to another. According to Sophie Leroy, a professor of organizational behavior at the University of Washington, it's not possible for us to seamlessly switch attention from one task to another. Leroy coined the term "attention residue" to describe the fragments of the previous task that remain in our

I've devoted an entire chapter later in the book to dealing with these distractions and interruptions, but here's a quick tip: one of the best things you can do for your productivity is launch the settings app on your phone and scroll through the notification settings for each app. Shut off all the ones that aren't absolutely necessary. Do the same on your computer and tablet if you frequently find your focus derailed as you use these devices. Which interruptions are truly important, and which are preventing you from getting past this forty-second mark? Most of them aren't worth it—this is why I've deleted email on my phone entirely.

---

* Another study looked at how often fifty people switched between tasks and examined the average focus duration of the ten most and least distracted participants. The most distracted multitaskers switched between tasks every twenty-nine seconds, and the least distracted participants switched between tasks every seventy-five seconds. In other words, the most focused participants barely worked for a minute before becoming distracted.

attentional space after we shift to another activity: "It could be that you're sitting in a meeting and your mind keeps going to a project you were working on right before the meeting, or something you anticipate doing right after the meeting. It's having that divided attention, where part of your brain is thinking about those other ongoing projects that you have. This is what makes it so difficult to devote yourself to what you're supposed to be doing in the present." This attention residue keeps our mind continuing to evaluate, problem-solve, reflect, and ruminate about a previous task long after we've transitioned to the next.

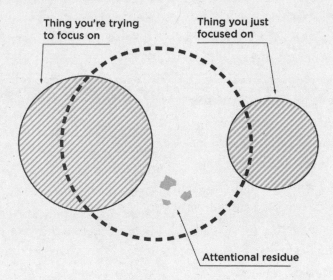

Switching becomes easier only once we finish a task—especially when time pressure, like a deadline, motivates us to get the task done. "By contrast," Leroy explains, "if you work on something and you don't really have to rush, but you get it done, your brain can keep thinking about 'What else should I have done?' or 'Is there another way to do this task?' or 'Maybe I could have done better.' Even though the task is completed, it's hard for your brain to get closure in general." Since our brain is no longer motivated to complete these loose-deadline tasks, Leroy found that "the mental activation of the goal [diminishes]." Time pressure narrows our focus on the task, restricting us from considering a number of more creative ways to complete it. We don't question our approach as much, because we haven't stepped back to consider the alternatives. This makes it easier to switch.

All this raises a question: Just how severe is the productivity cost of switching? Switching does make your work more stimulating, and its costs may be worth bearing if your work takes only 5 percent longer and you make only the occasional mistake. In practice, though, the cost is usually much greater. One study found that when we continually switch between tasks, **our work takes 50 percent longer, compared with doing one task from start to completion.** If you're working on a pressure- or deadline-free project, consider taking a break before starting something else so more of that attentional residue can dissipate. As far as your productivity is concerned, the best time to take a break is after you've finished a big task.

THE QUALITY OF YOUR ATTENTION

Intention is the bouncer of your attentional space—it lets in the productive objects of attention and keeps the distractions out. Few things will benefit your overall quality of life more than focusing with intention. It isn't possible to work and live with intention 100 percent of the time—demands get in the way, our focus shifts, and our attentional space overflows—but we can maintain our intention for enough of the day to accomplish a lot more than we would otherwise.

This chapter has been largely theoretical. In order to put its advice into practice, you'll need to do several things: set intentions more often, modify your environment to be less distracting, overcome the mental resistance you have to certain tasks, eliminate distractions *before* they derail you, and clear the distractions inside your own head. The subsequent chapters cover each of these ideas in turn, but understanding the principles behind them is essential.

Choosing where your attention is focused and maintaining a clear attentional space accomplishes several things at once. You will

- accomplish what you intend to much more often;
- focus more deeply, because you become a better defender of your attentional space;
- remember more, because you're able to more deeply process what you're doing;
- experience less guilt and doubt, knowing you've worked with intention;
- waste less time working on unimportant things;
- fall victim to fewer distractions—both external and internal;
- experience greater mental clarity, reduced stress, and fewer feelings of being overwhelmed;
- feel a stronger purpose behind your work, because you've chosen what's worthy of your attention (working with intention also prevents you from experiencing feelings of "dullness," which stem from having a lack of purpose); and
- develop deeper relationships and friendships as you spend more attention, not just time, with people.

There are numerous ways to measure the quality of your attention, but I've developed three measures to track my own progress. You can use these yardsticks to measure your progress as you adopt the tactics in this book into your life:

1. How much of your time you spend intentionally
2. How long you can hold your focus in one sitting
3. How long your mind wanders before you catch it

Now it's time to get tactical.

THE POWER OF HYPERFOCUS

INTRODUCING HYPERFOCUS

Think back to your last uber-productive work day, one when you accomplished a huge amount. On that day, chances are a number of things were true.

For starters, you were probably focusing on only one thing—maybe out of necessity, driven by a deadline. This one task filled your attentional space.

You were also likely able to dodge distractions and quickly got back on track every time an interruption did come up. While you were working with intense focus, you weren't working frantically, constantly switching between tasks. When your attention wandered—which it still did often, but less than usual—you quickly brought it back to the task at hand.

Your work was probably also at a comfortable level of difficulty: not so hard as to be intimidating; not so easy that it could be done out of habit. Because of this, you may have even become *completely* engrossed in your work, entering a "flow" state, where each time you looked at the clock another hour had flown by, even though you experienced that time as only fifteen minutes. Miraculously, you managed to accomplish the equivalent of several hours of work in each of them.

Finally, once you overcame the hurdle of getting started, you experienced little resistance to continuing. Even though you were working hard, you weren't exhausted afterward; curiously, you were less tired than after slower workdays. Your motivation remained strong even if you had to stop working because you got hungry or had a meeting or it was time to head home.

On this day you activated your brain's most productive mode: *hyperfocus.**

When you hyperfocus on a task, you expand one task, project, or other object of attention . . .

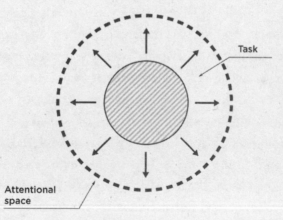

Task

Attentional
space

---

* This term originates in ADHD literature and describes the phenomenon when a single task consumes one's full attention, whether or not that task is important. It's not that those with ADHD can't focus—it's that it's more difficult for them to control when they do. I've adapted the term to have a similar meaning—intense focus, but coupled with deliberate attention. It doesn't matter how deeply you focus if what you're focusing on is not important.

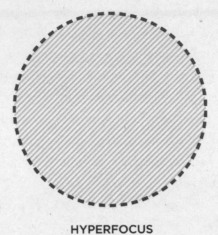

HYPERFOCUS

. . . so it fills your attentional space completely.

You enter this mode by managing your attention deliberately and purposefully: by choosing one important object of attention, eliminating distractions that will inevitably arise as you work, and then focusing on just that one task. Hyperfocus is many things at once: it's deliberate, undistracted, and quick to refocus, and it leads us to become completely immersed in our work. It also makes us immensely happy. Recall how energized you were by your work the last time you found yourself in this state. In hyperfocus you might even feel more relaxed than you usually are when you work. Allowing one task or project to consume your full attentional space means this state doesn't make you feel stressed or overwhelmed. Your attentional space doesn't overflow, and your work doesn't feel nearly as chaotic. Since hyperfocus is so much more productive, you can slow down a bit and still accomplish an incredible amount in a short period of time.

This mode may feel like an elusive luxury in the on-the-go environments in which we work and live today. But nothing could be further from the truth. Hyperfocus means you're *less* busy, because you're permitting fewer objects into your attentional space. Picking which tasks to work on ahead of time lets you focus on what's actually important in the moment. This has never been more crucial than in our knowledge-work environments, where not all tasks are created equal. You'll often accomplish more in one hour of hyperfocus than in an entire day spent filling your attentional space to the brim with multiple—and often undeliberate—concerns. This is counterintuitive but absolutely essential advice: the more demands made on your time, the more essential it becomes to choose what—and how many—things you pay attention to. **You're never too busy to hyperfocus.**

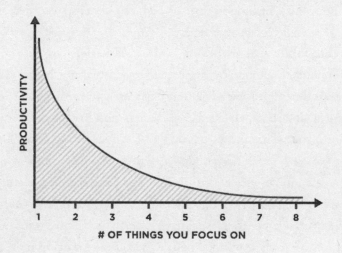

When it comes to your most important tasks, the fewer things you pay attention to, the more productive you become.

HYPERFOCUSING ON HABITS

The most important aspect of hyperfocus is that only one productive or meaningful task consumes your attentional space. This is simply nonnegotiable. Here's why: the most critical tasks, projects, and commitments benefit from every bit of extra attention. They're usually not habits, which by default don't often consume your full attentional space.

This is not to say it's impossible to hyperfocus on a habit. There is no task too small to consume your attention—if you tried hard enough, you could commit your complete attention to watching paint dry. But there are two reasons why this mental mode is best preserved for complex tasks, rather than habits.

First, hyperfocus requires willpower and mental energy to activate, drawing from the limited supply we have to make it through the day. Because habits consume so little of our attentional space, there's really no need to hyperfocus on them.

Second, and more interesting, while your performance on complex tasks benefits when you focus more completely, your habitual-task performance actually *suffers* when you focus with your total attention.

You may have experienced this the last time you noticed someone watching you walk, and you brought your focus to making sure you walked *like a perfectly normal human being*. Chances are you immediately started moving like a full-blown mechanical robot, feeling as if you were flailing all over the sidewalk. To put it bluntly, your walking performance suffered.* Or maybe the last time you went bowling you found yourself thinking about why you were scoring more points than usual—what exactly you were doing well. But then your opponents started pulling ahead and eventually won. You choked, and your performance suffered by your bringing your full attention to a game you usually play out of habit. Studies analyzing skilled typists found this same phenomenon: the more attention they brought to their

---

* This effect is partly due to what, in psychology circles, is known as the spotlight effect—where you think everyone's watching you when really, they couldn't care less.

typing, the slower they typed and the more mistakes they made. When doing such habitual tasks, it's best to not focus completely on what you're doing.

Save hyperfocus for your most complex tasks—things that will actually benefit from your complete attention, such as writing a report, mapping your team's budget, or having a meaningful conversation with a loved one.

A few marvelous things happen when you do so. First, because you're focusing on a single task, you likely have some attentional space to spare—enough that you are also able to keep your original intention in mind. As a result, you are less likely to be derailed by distractions and interruptions, because you have enough awareness to notice that they are about to derail you. And maybe most important, you have enough attention to also think deeply about the task as you work. This allows you to remember and learn more, get back on track when your mind wanders, and consider alternative approaches as you solve problems. All of this will save you an immense amount of time in completing the task. One of the best ways to get more done—and done faster—is by preventing yourself from focusing on things that aren't important.

THE FOUR STAGES OF HYPERFOCUS

In any given moment you're focused on either your external environment, the thoughts in your head, or both. Engaging solely with your external environment means you're effectively living on autopilot. You slip into this mode as you wait for the traffic light to change or find yourself bouncing around a loop of the same apps on your phone. When you're engaged only with the thoughts in your head, you're daydreaming. This can happen when you go on a quick walk without your phone, your mind wanders in the shower, or you go for a jog. You enter into hyperfocus when you engage *both* your thoughts and your external environment and direct them at one thing intentionally.*

So How Do We Enter Hyperfocus Mode?

The science suggests we pass through four states as we begin to focus. First, we're focused (and productive). Then, assuming we don't get distracted or interrupted, our mind begins to wander. Third, we make note of this mind wandering. This can take awhile, especially if we don't frequently check what is consuming our attentional space. (On average, we notice about five times an hour that our mind has wandered.) And fourth, we shift our focus back to our original object of attention.

The four stages of hyperfocus are modeled on this framework.

To hyperfocus, you must

1. choose a productive or meaningful object of attention;
2. eliminate as many external and internal distractions as you can;
3. focus on that chosen object of attention; and
4. continually draw your focus back to that one object of attention.

Setting an intention for what we plan to focus on is the most important step—the more productive and meaningful the task, the more productive and meaningful your actions become. For example, if you set your intention to focus on mentoring a new employee, automating

---

* In this way, hyperfocus is the state that precedes what Mihaly Csikszentmihalyi calls a "flow" state—the state where we're entirely absorbed in what we're doing and time passes at a much faster speed. As Csikszentmihalyi explains in *Flow*, when we're immersed in this state, "nothing else seems to matter." This is yet another reason why focusing on only one thing is essential: our odds of experiencing flow rise exponentially when several things aren't competing for our limited attention. Hyperfocus is the process that leads us to flow.

a repetitive task, or brainstorming a new product idea, you'll be infinitely more productive than if you work intention-free and in autopilot mode.

This same idea applies at home: the more meaningful our objects of focus, the more meaningful our life becomes. We experience the benefits of hyperfocus mode by setting such simple intentions as being present in a conversation with our partner or fully enjoying a meal with our family. We learn more, remember more, and process our actions more deeply—and our lives become more meaningful as a result. This first step to reaching hyperfocus mode is essential—intention absolutely has to precede attention.

The second step to reaching hyperfocus is eliminating as many internal and external distractions as possible. There's a simple reason we fall victim to distraction: in the moment, distractions are more attractive objects of attention than what we really ought to be doing. This is true both at work and at home. Email alerts that pop into the corner of our screen are usually more tempting than the task we're doing in another window; the TV behind our partner at the pub is usually more enticing than focusing on the conversation.

Distractions are infinitely easier to deal with in advance—by the time they appear, it's often already too late to defend our intention against them. *Internal* distractions must be tamed as well—including random (and sometimes cringeworthy) memories and thoughts that bubble up as we're trying to focus, the mental resistance we have to unappealing tasks (like doing taxes or cleaning the garage), and the times we want to focus but our mind wants to wander.

Third, hyperfocus becomes possible when we focus on our chosen object of attention for a predetermined amount of time. This involves hunkering down for a set period that is both comfortable and feasible. The more groundwork we lay in the first two steps of hyperfocus, the more deeply and confidently we can accomplish step three.

Fourth, and finally, hyperfocus is about drawing our attention back to the original object of attention when our mind wanders. I'll repeat this point frequently, as it's one of the most important ideas in this book: again, research shows that our mind wanders for 47 percent of the day. In other words, if we're awake for eighteen hours, we're engaged in what we're doing for just *eight* of them. It's normal for our mind to wander, but the key is to center it so we can spend time and attention on what's actually in front of us.

In addition, it takes an average of *twenty-two minutes* to resume working on a task after we're distracted or interrupted. We fare even worse when we interrupt or distract *ourselves*—in these cases, it takes *twenty-nine minutes* to return to working on the original task. The more often we assess what's occupying our attentional space, the quicker we're able to get back on track. Don't stress too much about this right now—we'll get to specifics later in the book.

The concept of hyperfocus can be summed up in a single tranquil sentence: keep one important, complex object of attention in your awareness as you work.

Choosing What to Focus On

Attention without intention is wasted energy. Intention should always precede attention—in fact, the two ideas pair perfectly. Intention setting allows us to decide how we should spend our time; focusing our attention on that task gets it done efficiently. The best way to become more productive is to choose what you want to accomplish before you begin working.

When we set intentions, it's important to remember that not all work tasks are created equal. Some tasks enable us to accomplish an incredible amount with every minute we spend on them. These include such goals as setting aside time to plan what main tasks you want to accomplish each day, mentoring a new employee who joined your team a month ago, and writing that book you've been meaning to for years. These tasks fall into the "necessary" and "purposeful" quadrants discussed in chapter 1. When you measure work in these quadrants against unnecessary and distracting tasks like attending useless meetings, catching up on your social media feeds, and repeatedly checking for new email, it's not hard to see which are more productive. When we don't choose which quadrants of tasks to spend time on, we fall into autopilot.

This is not to say that we can't "get by" in autopilot mode. By being ultraresponsive to the work that comes our way, we can stay on top of most of it and probably be productive enough to not lose our jobs. But autopilot also fails to progress our work in any meaningful way. I suspect you don't get paid simply to play the role of "traffic cop" by moving emails, conversations, and instant messages around. Such tasks, and answering unanticipated demands that come your way, are always necessary. But whenever possible, you should take an active role in *choosing* where you spend your time and attention.

> **If you haven't done so already,** this is a great time to create a 2 x 2 grid of your work—sorting your standard monthly tasks based on whether they're productive or unproductive and attractive or unattractive. The ironic thing about investing in your productivity is that it's almost impossible to do when you're slogging it out in the office trenches. There's simply too much to keep up with— meetings, email chains, and project deadlines included. For this reason, the best productivity tactics are the ones that require you to step back and remove yourself from your work so you have the mental space to think critically about

how you should approach that work differently. That way, when you return to work, you can do it more intelligently, instead of just harder. Figuring out your four types of work tasks is one of these "stepping back" activities. Now is the best time to do so—especially before you read the very next section. It'll take just five to ten minutes.

In researching attention and intention over the last few years, I've developed a few favorite daily intention-setting rituals. Here are my top three.

1. The Rule of 3

You can probably skim this section if you're familiar with material I've written in the past. If not, allow me to introduce the Rule of 3: **at the start of each day, choose the three things you want to have accomplished by day's end.** While a to-do list is useful to capture the minutiae of the day, these three intention slots should be reserved for your most important daily tasks.

I've done this little ritual every morning for several years, ever since learning about it from Microsoft's director of digital transformation, J. D. Meier. The Rule of 3 is deceptively simple. By forcing yourself to pick just three main intentions at the start of each day, you accomplish several things. You choose what's important but also what's *not* important—the constraints of this rule push you to figure out what actually matters. The rule is also flexible within the constraints of your day. If your calendar is packed with meetings, those commitments may dictate the scope of your three intentions, while an appointment-free day means you can set intentions to accomplish more important and less urgent tasks. When unexpected tasks and projects come your way, you can weigh those new responsibilities against the intentions you've already set. Because three ideas fit comfortably within your attentional space, you can recall and remember your original intentions with relative ease.

Make sure to keep your three intentions where you can see them—I keep mine on the giant whiteboard in my office or, if I'm traveling, at the top of my daily to-do list, which is synced between devices in OneNote. If you're like me, you may also find it handy to set three *weekly* intentions, as well as three daily *personal* intentions—such as disconnecting from work during dinner, visiting the gym before heading home from the office, or gathering receipts for taxes.

On days when your schedule is set—such as when you're attending a conference—you may not be able to determine how you spend your time and attention. You can, however, change *how you relate* to what you have to get done. For example, instead of making an intention to "attend conference talks," opt instead to "connect with five new people at the cocktail reception."

2. Your Most Consequential Tasks

A second intention-setting ritual I follow is considering which items on my to-do list are the most *consequential*.

If you have the habit of maintaining a to-do list (which I highly recommend and whose power I will discuss later in the book), take a second to consider the consequences of carrying out each task—the sum of both its short-term and long-term consequences. The most important tasks on your list are the ones that lead to the greatest positive consequences.

What will be different in the world—or in your work or in your life—as a result of your spending time doing each of the items on your list? What task is the equivalent of a domino in a line of one hundred that, once it topples over, initiates a chain reaction that lets you accomplish a great deal?

Another way to look at this: when deciding what to do, instead of considering just the immediate consequences of an activity, also consider the *second-* and *third-order* consequences. For example, let's say you're deciding whether to order a funnel cake for dessert. The immediate consequence of the decision is that you enjoy eating the cake. But the second- and third-order consequences are quite a bit steeper. A second-order consequence might be that you'll feel terrible for the rest of the evening. Third-order consequences might include gaining weight or breaking a new diet regimen.

This is a powerful idea to internalize, especially since the most important tasks are often not the ones that immediately *feel* the most urgent or productive. Writing a guide for new hires may not, in the moment, feel as valuable as answering a dozen emails, but if that guide cuts down on the time it takes to bring each new employee on board, makes her feel more welcome, and also serves to make her more productive, it is easily the most consequential thing on your list. Other consequential tasks might include automating a task that's annoying and repetitive, disconnecting so you can focus on designing the workflow for an app you're building, or forming an office mentorship program that lets employees easily share their knowledge.

If you have a lot of tasks on your to-do list, ask yourself: which are the most consequential? This exercise works well in tandem with the four types of tasks in your work. Once you've separated them into the four quadrants of necessary, purposeful, distracting, and unnecessary, ask yourself: Out of the necessary and purposeful tasks, which have the potential to set off a chain reaction?

3. The Hourly Awareness Chime

Setting three daily intentions and prioritizing your most consequential tasks are great ways to be more intentional every day and week. But how can you ensure you're working intentionally on a moment-by-moment basis?

As far as productivity is concerned, these individual moments are where the rubber meets the road—it's pointless to set goals and intentions if you don't act toward accomplishing them throughout the day. My favorite way to make sure I'm staying on track with my intentions is to frequently check what's occupying my attentional space—to reflect on whether I'm focusing on what's important and consequential or whether I've slipped into autopilot mode. To do so, I set an hourly awareness chime.

A key theme of *Hyperfocus* is that you shouldn't be too hard on yourself when you do notice your brain drifting off or doing something else weird. Your mind will always wander, so consider how that might present an opportunity to assess how you're feeling and then to set a path for what to do next. Research shows that we are more likely to catch our minds wandering when we reward ourselves for doing so. Even if you minimize one or two distractions and set just one or two intentions each day, you're doing better than most. If you're anything like me, your hourly awareness chime may at first reveal that you're usually not working on something important or consequential. That's okay—and even to be expected.

The important thing is that you're regularly checking what's occupying your attentional space. Set an hourly timer on your phone, smartwatch, or another device—this will easily be the most productive interruption you receive throughout the day.

When your hourly chime rings, ask yourself the following:

- Was your mind wandering when the awareness chime sounded?
- Are you working on autopilot or on something you intentionally chose to do? (It's so satisfying to see this improve over time.)
- Are you immersed in a productive task? If so, how long have you spent focusing on it? (If it was an impressive amount of time, don't let the awareness chime trip you up—keep going!)
- What's the most consequential thing you could be doing right now? Are you working on it?
- How full is your attentional space? Is it overflowing, or do you have attention to spare?
- Are there distractions preventing you from hyperfocusing on your work?

You don't have to answer all of these questions—pick two or three prompts that you find most helpful, ones that will make you refocus on what's important. Doing this hourly increases all three measures of attention quality: it helps you focus longer because you spot and prevent distractions on the horizon; you notice more often that your mind has wandered and can refocus it; and you can, over time, spend more of your day working intentionally.

When you first start this check-in, you probably won't fare so well and will find yourself frequently working on autopilot, getting distracted, and spending time on unnecessary and distracting tasks. That's fine! When you do, adjust course to work on a task that's more productive, and tame whatever distractions derailed you in that moment. If you notice the same distractions frequently popping up, make a plan to deal with them. (We'll do this in the next chapter.)

Try setting an hourly awareness chime for one workday this week. While at first the interruptions will admittedly be annoying, they'll establish a valuable new habit. If you don't like the idea of an awareness chime, try using a few cues in your environment that trigger you to think about what's occupying your attentional space. I no longer use an hourly awareness chime, though I found it to be the most helpful method to get into the practice. Today I reflect on what I've been working on during a few predetermined times: each time I walk to the washroom, when I leave my desk to get water or tea, or when my phone rings. (I answer the call after a few rings, once I've reflected on what was occupying my attentional space.)

HOW TO SET STRONGER INTENTIONS

Over the last few decades Peter Gollwitzer has been one of the most renowned contributors to the field of intention. He's perhaps best known for his groundbreaking research on the importance of not only setting intentions but also making them very specific. While we often achieve our vague intentions, specific intentions greatly increase our odds of overall success.

Let's say, for example, you rushed to set your personal intentions this morning and came up with this list:

1. Go to the gym.
2. Quit working when I get home.
3. Get to bed by a reasonable time.

I've deliberately made these intentions vague, but how can we make them more specific and likely to stick?

First, it's worth considering how effective these intentions are as I've formulated them. They will certainly prove to be more effective than doing nothing. In fact, Gollwitzer's research discovered that even vague intentions like these boost your odds of successfully carrying them out by around 20 percent to 30 percent. So, if you're lucky, you might cross another one or two off the list. Not bad!

Setting more specific intentions, however, does something remarkable: it makes our odds of success much higher. In one study, Gollwitzer and his research colleague Veronika Brandstätter asked participants to set an intention to complete a difficult goal over Christmas break—such as completing a term paper, finding a new apartment, or settling a conflict with their significant other. Some students set a vague intention while others set what Gollwitzer calls an "implementation intention." As he explains the term: "Make a very detailed plan on how you want to achieve what you want to achieve. What I'm arguing in my research is that goals need plans, ideally plans that include when, where, and which kind of action to move towards the goal." In other words, if a student's vague goal was to "find an apartment during Christmas break," his implementation intention could be "I will hunt for apartments on Craigslist and email three apartment landlords in the weeks leading up to Christmas."

Comparing Gollwitzer and Brandstätter's two participant groups is where things get interesting. A remarkable *62 percent* of students who set a specific implementation intention followed through on their goals. The group that did not set an implementation intention fared a lot more poorly, following through on their original intention *a third as often*—a paltry 22 percent of the time. This effect, which subsequent studies validated further, was positively staggering. **Setting specific intentions can double or triple your odds of success**.

With that in mind, let's quickly turn my three vague intentions into implementation intentions:

1. "Go to the gym" becomes "Schedule and go to the gym on my lunch break."
2. "Quit working when I get home" is reframed as "Put my work phone on airplane mode and my work laptop in another room, and stay disconnected for the evening."

3. "Get to bed by a reasonable time" becomes "Set a bedtime alarm for 10:00 p.m., and when it goes off, start winding down."

Implementation intentions are powerful in much the same way as habits. When you begin a habit, your brain carries out the rest of the sequence largely on autopilot. Once you have a game plan for an implementation intention, when you encounter the environmental cue to initiate it—your lunch break rolls around, you get home after a stressful day at work, or your bedtime alarm goes off—you subconsciously get the ball rolling to accomplish your goals. Your intentions take almost no effort to initiate. As Gollwitzer and Brandstätter put it, "action initiation becomes swift, efficient, and does not require conscious intent." In other words, we begin to act toward our original goal automatically.

Gollwitzer told me that the intentions do not necessarily have to be precise if they are specific enough for a person to understand and identify the situational cues: "We did studies with tennis players, and they made plans on how they want to respond with the problems that might come up in the game. Some of the tennis players were specifying 'when I get irritated' or 'when I get nervous.' That is not very specific or concrete, but it worked brilliantly because they knew what they meant with 'nervous.' Specific means the person can identify the critical situation."

There are two notable caveats to setting specific intentions. First, you have to actually care about your intentions. Implementation intentions don't work nearly as well for goals that don't especially matter to you or that you've long abandoned. If you had a goal in the 1990s to amass the world's largest collection of Furbys, you'll probably be a lot less motivated to achieve that goal today.

Second, easy-to-accomplish intentions don't have to be as specific. Deciding in advance when you'll work on a task is significantly more

important for a difficult one than when your intention is to do something simple. If it's the weekend, and your intention is to go to the
gym at least once, you don't need to be as definite about when you'll
do so. If you're trying to accomplish something more challenging,
though, like saying no to dessert at the restaurant on Saturday, setting a more specific intention is essential. That vague intention can
become more specific by planning, when you see the dessert menu, to
politely decline and treat yourself to a decaf coffee instead. This caveat
works well for intentions at home, but when Monday rolls around,
you may need to again set more thoughtful intentions. "When the
goals are tough, or when you have so many goals and it's hard to attain them all, that's when planning works particularly well," Gollwitzer adds.

STARTING A HYPERFOCUS RITUAL

The next chapter focuses on taming the external and internal distractions that inevitably derail hyperfocus. However, before discussing
these, I want to offer a few simple strategies to begin hyperfocusing on
your intentions. These will become infinitely more powerful as you
learn to tame the distractions in your work in advance.

Let's first cover how to focus, and then when. Both ideas are pretty
simple.

How to hyperfocus:

- **Start by "feeling out" how long you want to hyperfocus.** Have a
  dialogue with yourself about how resistant you feel toward the
  mode, particularly if you're about to hunker down on a difficult,
  frustrating, or unstructured task. As an example: "Do I feel comfortable focusing for an hour? No way. Forty-five minutes? Better,

but still no. Thirty minutes? That's doable, but still . . . Okay, twenty-five minutes? Actually, I could probably do that." It's incredibly rewarding to experience your hyperfocus time limit increase over time. Push yourself—but not too hard. When I started practicing hyperfocus, I began with fifteen-minute blocks of time, each punctuated by a five- to ten-minute distraction break. Hyperfocusing all day would be a chore, and a few stimulating distractions are always fun, especially at first. You'll soon become accustomed to working with fewer distractions.

- **Anticipate obstacles ahead of time.** If I know I have a busy few days coming up, at the beginning of the week I like to schedule my hyperfocus periods—several chunks of time throughout the week that I'll use to focus on something important. This way, I make sure to carve out time to hyperfocus, instead of getting swept up in last-minute tasks and putting out proverbial fires. Such planning lets my coworkers and assistant know not to book me during these times, and it also reminds me when I'm committed to focus. In weeks like these, a few minutes of advance planning can save hours of wasted productivity.

- **Set a timer.** I usually use my phone for this, which might sound ironic, given the distractions it can bring. If these phone distractions will cause a focus black hole, either put it on airplane mode or use a watch or other timer.

- **Hyperfocus!** When you notice that your mind has wandered or that you've gotten distracted, bring your attention back to your intention. Again, don't be too tough on yourself when this happens—this is the way your brain is wired to work. If you feel like going for longer when your timer rings—which you probably will because you'll be on a roll—don't stop.

That covers the *how*. Here are a few suggestions that I have found work for deciding *when* you should hyperfocus:

- **Whenever you can!** Naturally, we need time for the little things, but the more you can hyperfocus, the better. Throughout the week, you should schedule as many blocks of time to hyperfocus as your work will allow, and for as long as you personally feel comfortable. We're the most productive and happy when we work on one meaningful thing at a time, so there's no reason not to spend as much time in this mode as we possibly can. Whenever you have an important task or project and a window in which you can work on it, don't pass up the opportunity to hyperfocus—you'll be missing out on a lot of productivity if you do. Naturally, because of the nature of our jobs, we often have to do a lot of collaborative work, which necessitates our being available to our colleagues. But when you're working on a task that only you can do, it's the perfect time to enter into hyperfocus mode.

- **Around the constraints of your work.** Most of us don't have the luxury of hyperfocusing whenever we wish. Productivity is often a process of understanding our constraints. On most days we will be able to find a few opportunities to hyperfocus, and on others it simply won't be possible. I find the latter to be especially the case while traveling, when I'm at a conference, or when I have a day full of exhausting meetings. Make sure you account for time and energy constraints—and if possible, work around these obstacles when you're planning your week.

- **When you need to work on a complex task.** While I started hyperfocusing by scheduling blocks of time into my calendar, I now enter into the mode whenever I'm working on a complex task or project that will benefit from my full attention. If I'm just checking my email, I won't set an intention to hyperfocus, but if I'm writing, planning a talk, or attending an important meeting, I invariably do.

- **Based on how averse you are to what you intend to accomplish.** The more aversive you find a task or project, the more important it is to tame distractions ahead of time. You're most likely to procrastinate on tasks that you consider boring, frustrating, difficult, ambiguous, or unstructured, or that you don't find rewarding or meaningful. In fact, if you call to mind something you're putting off doing, chances are it has most of these characteristics. The more aversive a task, the more important it is that we enter into a hyperfocused state so we can work on the task with intention.

BUILDING YOUR FOCUS

Over the next several chapters, I'll give you the tools you need to develop your focus. As you'll find, your ability to hyperfocus depends on a few factors, all of which affect the quality of your attention:

- How frequently you seek out new and novel objects of attention. (This is often why we initially resist a hyperfocus ritual.)
- How often you habitually overload your attentional space.
- How frequently your attention is derailed by interruptions and distractions.
- How many tasks, commitments, ideas, and other unresolved issues you're keeping in your head.
- How frequently you practice meta-awareness (checking what's already consuming your attention).

As we'll discuss, even your mood and diet can influence hyperfocus. For these reasons and more, everyone has a different starting point when it comes to entering the mode.

Ironically, when I first started exploring the research on how we best manage our attention, I could hardly focus for more than a few minutes before becoming distracted. This is often the case when we continually seek novel objects of attention and work in a distracting environment.

While experimenting with the research, I've been able to steadily increase the amount of time I can hyperfocus, and I've grown accustomed to working with fewer distractions. I wrote the sentence you're now reading near the end of a forty-five-minute hyperfocus session—my third of the day. These sessions have enabled me to write exactly 2,286 words in around two hours. (This is one of the fun parts about writing a book about productivity: you can verify that your methods actually work by using them to write the book itself.) The third session was my last hyperfocus block, and between those periods I caught up on email, enjoyed checking social media, and had a quick chat with a coworker or two.

But right now isn't one of those times. And focusing on just one thing—writing these words—is what has allowed me to be so productive over the last forty-five minutes. It'll work for you too.

CHAPTER 4

TAMING DISTRACTIONS

FORTY SECONDS

Two fascinating experts I had the chance to speak with while writing this book were Gloria Mark and Mary Czerwinski. Mark is a professor of information science at the University of California at Irvine and is perhaps the world's foremost expert on attention and multitasking. She has conducted attentional studies in partnership with NASA and with companies like Boeing, Intel, IBM, and Microsoft. Czerwinski, a principal researcher at Microsoft, is one of the leading experts on how people and computers interact.* Her work, and my conversations with her, color most of this chapter. The two scientists have teamed up to conduct scores of studies into our relationship with technology on a daily basis.

What I love the most about their work is that they specialize in what is called *in situ* research, conducting studies in actual workplaces on real workers. To measure how stressed participants felt after multitasking or doing email, Mark and Czerwinski strapped monitors

---

* Microsoft does a surprising amount of research—at this writing, it employs over two thousand people who do, and publish, research full time.

to them to wear twenty-four hours a day to chart their heart-rate variability—a scientifically validated measure of stress. With their permission, Mark and Czerwinski installed a logging program on participants' computers to observe exactly how often they switched between tasks—every forty seconds. Shockingly, we interrupt ourselves even more often when we keep apps like IM and Skype open—every *thirty-five* seconds.

Their work is worth calling out for a number of reasons. First, in situ research is much more difficult to conduct—it took Mark *six years* to find an organization that would let her study employees when they went without email for a week, for example—but the approach is particularly worthwhile. As she explained to me, "As opposed to taking someone into a laboratory and setting up artificial conditions to simulate the world, you're going *into* the world, and observing things as they actually are."

Second, their research is worth examining because it's groundbreaking. By far my favorite of the studies they conducted was the forty-second task-switching finding I cited above. So often we go from being totally productive and immersed in our work to interrupting ourselves to do something unrelated and far less important. We interrupt a meaningful conversation with a friend to check our phone; we set aside writing a report to initiate a pointless IM chat; we stop building an Excel worksheet to visit with an office colleague for no good reason.

Another study they conducted found that we switch between computer applications *566 times* during the average workday. This figure includes distractions that have nothing to do with our work itself—we check Facebook, for example, an average of 21 times a day. (This average includes every subject in the study, some of whom didn't look at Facebook at all. When you calculate the average among people who visited Facebook at least once, it almost doubles, to 38 daily checks.)

Our work obviously suffers from these distractions, and we fail to enter into a hyperfocused state. We compensate by working faster and more frantically, which affects the quality of what we produce and stresses us out. And perhaps most important, we fail to take control of, and deliberately manage, our attention.

Interruptions that are in some way related to a project we're working on don't derail our productivity as severely if someone sends us a message with information relevant to a report we're preparing, for example, we can refocus with relative ease. But we rarely have just one project on our plate—on average, we're juggling about ten simultaneously.

Your email and message notifications may be worth keeping on if you and your team are collaborating on the same project in crunch mode, but under most circumstances this isn't the case. The costs of an unrelated interruption can be massive: it takes an average of *twenty-five minutes* to resume working on an activity after we're interrupted, and before resuming that activity, we work on an average of 2.26 other tasks. We don't simply attend to the distraction or interruption and then return to the original task—we become distracted *a second time* before doing so.*

Once you become aware of how frequently you interrupt yourself, it's hard to go back to working the same way again. This is why it is critical to manage your attentional space wisely. You can focus for so much longer by taming distractions ahead of time.†

---

* Distractions become even costlier after the age of forty. Your attentional space shrinks as you age, which makes it more difficult to get back on track. Impressively, though your attentional space shrinks as you get older, your mind actually wanders *less*. The system in our brain that processes information dwindles as we age—this makes us less likely to fall victim to one distraction after another.

† One question that comes up frequently in attentional research is how women and men differ when it comes to multitasking. Women experience fewer interruptions and interrupt *themselves* less overall. And they do so while working on more projects at once. Compared with men, women are also happier and more engaged in the workplace.

WHY WE LOVE DISTRACTIONS

There is a simple reason why we fall victim to distractions. Even though we know they're unproductive, in the moment they are much more enticing than our work. When our brain is even slightly resisting a task, it hunts for more attractive things it could do instead.

Let your mind be for a few seconds, and you'll find that it gravitates to more captivating (and usually less important) objects of attention than what you should be focusing on.

We can't even go to the bathroom anymore without mindlessly distracting ourselves. I'd genuinely love to see how the duration of our bathroom breaks has changed over time—I'd wager a guess that they've at least doubled now that we carry around smartphones.*

Our drive toward distractions is made worse by our brain's built-in novelty bias and the fact that the websites and apps we frequent offer a hit of mindless stimulation and validation each time we visit them. You probably have a few notifications waiting each time you open Twitter—who shared your last post, new people who have followed you, and so on. It's hard to resist the urge to check the site throughout the day, knowing another small hit of validation is just a click away. Even if you have no messages waiting, the possibility that you *could* have some draws you back. I deleted my Facebook account a few years ago for this very reason.

I'm typing these words in one window on my computer screen, but I know that, in no time at all, it's possible to open another that could provide hours of distraction. Writing is a difficult task that my brain resists. I love the result, but the process takes a lot more focus and

---

* Something that's gone *down* since the introduction of the smartphone? Chewing gum sales. Since 2007—the year the iPhone was introduced—gum sales have plummeted 17 percent. Obviously correlation doesn't imply causation, but it does make you wonder.

energy than checking social media, answering email, or checking the news. If I don't disable computer distractions ahead of time, I might as well wave good-bye to my productivity.

As a small experiment, I didn't block any distractions on my computer this morning. Left to my own devices, I bounced around an endless loop of stimulating websites for thirty minutes. Looking at my browsing history, I had visited

- Twitter;
- Reddit (specifically the mechanical keyboard "subreddit");
- several news websites, including Feedly, *The New York Times*, CNN, *The Verge*, and MacRumors;
- my second Twitter account;
- email (I have three email accounts and checked them each a time or two); and
- the Amazon page for my first book, to check how well it was selling and to see if it had any new customer reviews.

It's also worth noting that I checked these websites *after* meditating for twenty-five minutes—a ritual that usually enables me to act with more intention. Chances are you have your own list of distracting websites and apps you frequent when you're resisting a task.*

The above anecdote alone should dispel any notion that, as a productivity expert, I have a superhuman level of self-control. What I *am* better at is managing my impulses *ahead of time*. After choosing how long you'll focus, eliminating distractions is the second step of hyperfocus. Eliminating distractions before you hunker down on a task

---

* Curiously, the distractions you're most likely to fall victim to differ depending on what you're working on. When you're doing rote work, you're significantly more likely to visit Facebook or initiate a face-to-face interaction with a coworker. When you're focused on more complex work, you're more likely to check your email.

makes focusing infinitely easier, as important tasks fill your attentional space quite naturally when there is nothing competing with them. Given that distractions have the potential to derail our productivity so frequently, and for so long, it's imperative that we deal with them ahead of time—before we have to expend precious willpower to resist their allure.

THE FOUR TYPES OF DISTRACTIONS

In chapter 1 I introduced the four types of work tasks: productive tasks that are either necessary or purposeful, and unproductive tasks that are either unnecessary or distracting. In this section, we'll focus on the distracting tasks that are fun and unproductive.

I define a "distraction" as anything that can direct us away from our intentions. In this respect, distractions and interruptions are much the same thing, because they both distance us from what we intend to accomplish. Some interruptions are essential—such as a piece of information you receive that's related to what you're working on in that moment. But most of them are worth taming ahead of time.

If we zoom in on the "distracting work" quadrant back in the first chapter, we can divide it up based on two criteria: whether or not we have control over the distractions and whether we find them annoying or fun.

If you allocated your professional activities into the four-types-of-work grid in chapter 1, use the tasks in the distracting quadrant as a starting point to fill out the grid on the next page. There will be a number of items to add—your distractions grid should contain every single thing, no matter how small, that draws you away from your intentions in the moment. It should also include distractions that aren't specifically work related—such as the news and social media websites you visit as you work. I won't ask you to do many exercises as you read

FOUR TYPES OF DISTRACTIONS/INTERRUPTIONS

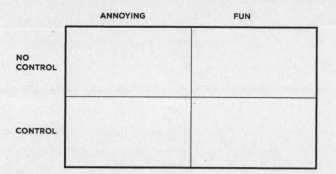

	ANNOYING	FUN
NO CONTROL		
CONTROL		

this book, but when I do include them, it's definitely for a good reason. (I've uploaded printable versions of both charts to this book's website: hyperfocusbook.com.)

To illustrate what a filled-out grid looks like, here are the typical distractions that throw off my intentions throughout the course of a day:

FOUR TYPES OF DISTRACTIONS/INTERRUPTIONS

	ANNOYING	FUN
NO CONTROL	- Office visitors - Loud colleagues - Meetings	- Team lunches - Calls from loved ones - Watercooler conversations
CONTROL	- Email - Phone alerts - Meetings	- News websites - Social media accounts - Instant messaging accounts

Let's start with the top two quadrants—how to deal with distractions and interruptions that we *can't* control.

There are two places from which distractions originate—ourselves and others—and both are important to deal with ahead of time. We can't prevent all distractions from arising—even if we closed our office door with the intent to hyperfocus for a couple of hours, we'd still receive phone calls and the occasional knock at the door. Many distractions are preventable, but many aren't, at least not without incurring large social costs. Research shows, however, that we interrupt ourselves just as much as we are interrupted by other people.* As Gloria Mark expressed it, "Simply looking at how we can break off external interruptions really only solves half the problem."

Distractions from others aren't quite as damaging as the times we interrupt ourselves. It takes us an average of twenty-nine minutes to resume a task after we have interrupted our own work—however, we get back on track around seven minutes more quickly if we're interrupted by someone else. Whether it's twenty-nine minutes or twenty-two minutes, we're still missing out on a lot of productivity. This is one of myriad reasons why periodically checking what's occupying our attentional space is so helpful. When we notice distractions have veered us off course, we waste less time on distracting tasks and get back on track more quickly.

While we can't prevent interruptions from arising, we can control how we respond to them. The best way to deal with annoying tasks that we can't keep from hijacking our attentional space—office visitors, loud colleagues, and unnecessary meetings included—is to keep our original intention in mind and get back to working on it as soon as possible.

We should also be more deliberate about how we respond to the *fun*

---

* This isn't the case if you're a manager or team leader, however—in this case, 60 percent of your interruptions come from others.

distractions we can't control. Of all the advice I offer in this book, this is the tactic I've struggled with the most. I'm often so gung-ho in accomplishing my intentions that I become rigid and grumpy when I'm interrupted—regardless of how enjoyable the interruption might be. As I've found, though, the best possible way to respond to pleasurable, controllable distractions—like team lunches and calls from loved ones when I'm in the middle of something—is to make a concerted effort to embrace and actually allow myself to *enjoy* them but still get back on track when I'm able. Fretting over things you simply can't control is a waste of time, energy, and attention. I've gradually learned to use these interruptions as a cue to lighten up a bit and embrace whatever fun derailed my productivity—while periodically recalling my original intention so I can get back on track when I have the opportunity.

DISTRACTION-FREE MODE

Most distractions fall into the category of ones we actually *can* control, which should therefore be tamed in advance.

FOUR TYPES OF DISTRACTIONS/INTERRUPTIONS

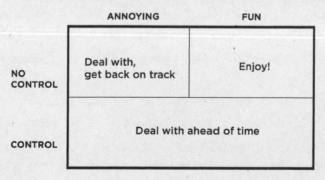

	ANNOYING	FUN
NO CONTROL	Deal with, get back on track	Enjoy!
CONTROL	Deal with ahead of time	

Over time, I've developed two modes of working:

1. A distraction-free mode, which I enter whenever I'm about to hyperfocus.
2. A regular, reduced-distraction working mode, where I work with a manageable number of distractions throughout the day.

Over the course of the day, we alternate between doing two types of work: focus work and collaborative work. Focus work benefits from all the attention we can bring to it—the less we're distracted, the more deeply we're able to focus, and the more productive we become. This allows us, as author Cal Newport has put it, to do "deep work."

Collaborative work, on the other hand, involves interacting with other people and being available in case you're needed. The more you and your team are available for one another, the more productive your team as a whole becomes. When engaged in collaborative work, it's best to enter into reduced-distraction mode, in which you've tamed your largest distractions but are still accessible when you're needed.

The breakdown of how much focus and collaborative work you do varies depending on your job. If you're an administrative assistant, your work may involve 90 percent collaboration and 10 percent focus work. If you're a writer, your work may require 90 percent focus work and 10 percent collaboration. Ask yourself: Roughly what breakdown does your job have overall?

Let's tackle the more intense, distraction-free mode first.

Creating a distraction-free mode enables you to eliminate almost every controllable distraction in advance so you can hyperfocus on your most important tasks. **By removing every object of attention that's potentially more stimulating and attractive than what**

you intend to do, you give your brain no choice but to work on that task.

I'm writing these words in my own distraction-free mode. To enter this mode and hyperfocus, I . . .

- launch a distraction-blocking app on my computer, which prevents me from accessing the websites that derail my productivity—email, social media sites, Amazon, and every other app and website I've specified on a block list. I specify the duration of time I want to hyperfocus, and if I do want to access any blocked sites during that period, I have to *physically restart my computer*. Since most of my work is done on a computer, this is easily the most important measure I take. I also put my computer in "do not disturb" mode so I'm not distracted as notifications come in;

- put my phone in "do not disturb" mode and keep it out of sight or in another room so I'm not tempted to check it;

- grab a coffee if I'm not going to bed in the next ten hours (again, it takes caffeine an average of eight to fourteen hours to metabolize out of your system); and

- put on noise-canceling headphones so I'm not distracted by sounds in my environment. I don't always use them in my office or if I'm working out of a hotel room, but I'll do so without fail if I'm hyperfocusing on a plane or at a coffee shop.

Which distractions derail your productivity over the course of a day? How many of them can you disable simultaneously with a blocking app or some other tactic? Write a quick plan, like the one above, that will guide you in dealing with these distractions ahead of time.

When you find your attention getting derailed, reflect on what caused it so you can disable that distraction the next time around—for example, when I'm distracted by a new website or app while in my distraction-free mode, I'll immediately add that site to my block list.

Here are a few more suggestions for creating your distraction-free mode:

- **There are many apps available that cut you off from distractions.** A few of my favorites for computer are Freedom (paid, though there's a free trial—Windows, Mac, iPhone, iPad), Cold Turkey (free, though there's a paid version—Windows, Mac, Android), and RescueTime (paid, though there's a free trial—PC, Mac, Android, Linux). Most of these cost a few dollars a month for the pro version, but you'll earn that money back in increased productivity. The research backs this up: people who deploy distraction blockers are more productive and focus for longer periods of time.

- **If your workplace restricts what apps or plug-ins you can install on your computer,** consider either unplugging the Ethernet cable or completely shutting off your computer's WiFi. This sounds extreme, but we spend a lot of our internet time procrastinating.

- **Get out of the office.** If you work in a more flexible office environment, you might find

We're only beginning to understand how traits such as conscientiousness, neuroticism, and impulsiveness work together to determine how distractible we are. These traits also determine how much stress the use of distraction blockers may cause. If you find you become anxious with a blocker enabled, you may decide that you want to resort to using it only when you're working on a task that's especially onerous or when you have less energy (and therefore less of an ability to resist distractions).

a distraction-free mode can incorporate working out of the coffee shop downstairs or in a meeting room.

- **Be thoughtful and don't underestimate (or overestimate) the social costs of your distraction-free mode.** Consider the effects of shutting yourself off from your coworkers, especially if your workplace is a social environment. At the same time, don't *over*estimate the social costs: while you might feel guilty closing your email client for thirty minutes, remember that your clients and coworkers frequently wait an hour or two for you to respond when you're caught in meetings. This is a lesson I'm relearning constantly: as a general rule, your coworkers need you a lot less than you think they do.

- **Treat yourself.** After I've completed a hyperfocus session and I leave my distraction-free mode, I'll occasionally treat myself to an all-you-can-eat buffet of distractions. Research shows that the more impulsive you are, the more stressed you become by blocking yourself from distractions. If you do have little self-control, or if you're impulsive, indulging in the odd distraction break can be beneficial. (Side note: impulsiveness is also the character trait most highly correlated with procrastination.) I also usually indulge a cup of matcha or coffee before entering back into my distraction-free mode, which positively reinforces my behavior to focus more deeply.

- **Create a distraction-free mode for your team.** Dale Partridge, author of *People Over Profit*, went as far as to equip his team with lamps and squirt guns to encourage them to focus when he was CEO of Sevenly. As he explained to me, "One of the smartest things I did at Sevenly was to build custom walnut desk lamps for the entire team. They turned them on whenever they wanted to focus, and the rule was that no one was allowed to interrupt them when their lamp was on. All forty-five employees were allowed to have up to three hours of uninterrupted focus time per day—we had to limit it because that uninterrupted time was so addictive! I also equipped everyone with a squirt gun they could spray each other with when they were interrupted."

The intensity of your distraction-free mode depends on your work environment. If you work for yourself or have an office with a door, you likely have more flexibility in eliminating distractions. If you work in a collaborative open-office environment, however, you may not be able to set up as strong a distraction-free mode as you'd like. Productivity is a process of understanding and adapting to your constraints.

I always experience an odd and wonderful sense of relief when I enter my distraction-free mode, and I think you will too. Suddenly you don't have to tend to the news, your social media feeds, and a never-ending stream of email. You can relax, confident that you can no longer waste time and attention on mindless busywork. You accomplish meaningful work and hyperfocus for a longer period of time. And you know that because you're investing your time, attention, and energy into just one task, you can slow down and work more purposefully.

A distraction-free mode also allows you to conserve energy. When you eliminate distractions, your energy goes further, and you can work for longer periods without needing a break. By disabling distractions ahead of time, you expend significantly less mental energy regulating your behavior in order to focus on your work. In turn, the less we have to regulate our behavior—when we don't have to battle distractions or watch what we say as we deal with a difficult coworker—the more energy our work provides. Breaks are energizing for this same reason—they're a pocket of time in which we can press pause on regulating our behavior. You may find that even though you intended to hyperfocus for only a short amount of time, you have the energy to keep going long after.

A distraction-free mode is especially valuable after a vacation or long weekend, as during these periods you'll have less energy and be more susceptible to distraction. Taming the distractions in your work ahead of time enables you to build up your energy as you settle back into your regular working rhythm.

WORKING WITH REDUCED DISTRACTIONS

Because it's impossible to work in hyperfocus mode 100 percent of the time, we should also learn to enjoy the benefits of cutting back on distractions during other periods of our day. To figure out which ones are worth taming, ask yourself: What distractions interrupt your focus throughout the day that aren't worth losing twenty or more minutes of productivity over? It isn't possible to shut off these distractions entirely, and you might not even want to, but it is worth becoming more thoughtful about what interrupts your work.

Email is a great example of a distraction that's important to tame but not eliminate. Email is a weird beast: it consumes a lot more attention than it does time. (Meetings are the opposite, generally consuming more time than attention.) Eliminating email would obviously not be realistic, but try to become more deliberate about when you check for messages. Doing so will allow you to regain control over your attention. Whenever you have email notifications enabled, you permit your coworkers to interrupt your focus on a whim—the instant you receive an email notification, you've lost control. Choosing when you check for messages ahead of time means you maintain control over your attention and resist slipping into autopilot mode.

Setting a specific time to focus on distractions like email, meetings, your smartphone, and social media transforms them from distractions into merely other purposeful elements of your work and life. Technology should exist for our convenience, not for the convenience of anyone who wants to interrupt us. Countless things clamor for our attention over the course of a day. Below I've chosen five of the most common pain points: a constant flood of notifications; smartphones (and other distracting devices); email; meetings; and, finally, the internet.

Notifications

An activity I recommended earlier in this book was to scroll through the notification settings on all of your devices and disable audible and vibrating alerts for interruptions you can safely live without. Leaving default settings turned on will flood you with a *constant* stream of interruptions. It's also worth limiting certain apps to interrupting you on only one device—there's no reason for your phone, tablet, watch, and computer to all inform you that you've received an email notifying you that your favorite clothing store is having a sale.

Disabling most audible and vibrating alerts is a simple change but one that's totally profound in practice: you suddenly get to choose when you're interrupted by your phone, rather than your phone deciding when to interrupt you. I personally just scan for new text messages and notifications when I check the clock on my phone.

Every notification pulls you away from what you're doing and reminds you there's an entire digital world you're missing out on. Notifications are deceiving, for while it takes just a second to glance at one, that moment can suck you into a digital vortex in which you easily lose a half hour of your time and attention. Not many notifications are worth this productivity drain.

That said, many notifications *are* worth receiving 100 percent of the time—phone calls, for example. While I check my email just once a day—as I'll discuss below—I'll often turn on a notification for just one sender if I'm waiting for an important message. Doing this takes a minute or two, but I easily earn that time back in how much more deeply I'm able to focus. This lets me stop worrying and compulsively checking my inbox every few minutes. Setting up your email to receive notifications only for a group of "VIP senders" is also possible in most email applications and lets you decide who can interrupt you throughout the day.

As well as dealing with individual notifications, it's also possible to block *when* you allow apps to distract you. One of my favorite daily rituals is to put my smartphone and other devices in airplane mode between 8:00 p.m. and 8:00 a.m. This is when I have the least energy and am more likely to fall victim to distractions. Plus, research shows we're less likely to multitask when we end our daily activities and go to bed early the night before. If enabling airplane mode feels too drastic, consider enabling your phone's "do not disturb" mode while you work.

Your Smartphone (and Other Devices)

Apart from managing the notifications that your devices pop up, it's worth becoming deliberate about when, where, and how often you use those devices.

Your phone is probably your most stimulating and novel object of attention, and you're absolutely going to be tempted by it, especially when the task you're working on becomes more intimidating or complex. Over time, I've changed my relationship with my phone—instead of seeing it as a device that should stay attached to my hip for the entire day, I've started to regard it as a powerful, more annoying computer. Their cellular radios aside, our phones have the same parts as a computer—but for some reason, perhaps because they provide us with so much stimulation and validation throughout the day, we allow them to interrupt us constantly, infinitely more than our computers. We shouldn't give any shiny rectangular device so much power.

Once I began viewing my smartphone as just a more distracting computer, I kept it stowed in my laptop bag instead of my pocket. And, most important, I made sure I had a good reason before checking it. This shift in attitude has enabled me to use my phone with intention, rather than on autopilot mode. Every time you pick up your phone without intent, you derail your attention for no good reason.

Here are a few more strategies to prevent your phone (and other devices) from taking over your life:

- **Mind the gaps.** Resist the urge to tap around on your smartphone when you're waiting in line at the grocery store, walking to the coffee shop, or in the bathroom. Use these small breaks to reflect on what you're doing, to recharge, and to consider alternate approaches to your work and life. In these moments, mindlessly burning time on the phone isn't worth it—doing so eliminates the valuable space in your schedule.

- **Do a phone swap.** Swap phones with a good friend or significant other when you're at dinner or hanging out. That way, if you have to look something up, make a call, or take a picture, you'll have a device to do it with—but one that won't suck you into a personalized world of distraction.

- **Strategically use airplane mode.** Flip your phone into airplane mode when working on an important task or having coffee with someone. It's impossible to share quality time without also sharing quality attention. Enabling airplane mode makes a bigger difference than merely putting your phone in your pocket, as in the latter case you're still aware that notifications and distractions are piling up and waiting for you. Airplane mode completely eliminates the possibility that a notification will disrupt your work. You can then deal with these alerts on your own terms later.

- **Buy a second "distractions" device.** This may sound a bit silly, but I recently bought an iPad that I use for one sole purpose: as a distractions device. I keep few social media apps (and no email app) on my phone and instead use my iPad for all things distracting. Delegating those tasks to the iPad—which I leave in another room—lets me focus for longer, and more deeply, in the event I do need to keep my smartphone by my side. Buying a tablet for this sole purpose is a sizable investment at first, but your attention is worth it.

- **Create a "Mindless" folder.** Try housing your most distracting apps—the ones that pull you into autopilot mode—in a "Mindless" folder on your phone or tablet. The folder's name will serve as an additional reminder that you're about to distract yourself.

- **Prune your list of apps.** Scroll through your phone and delete the apps on which you waste too much time and attention—social media and news apps included. Doing so can feel oddly refreshing, a sort of spring cleaning for your phone. Consider which apps duplicate functionality with those on your other devices. Your email app may not be worth keeping if you also access email on your tablet; an investment app you check compulsively might be worth deleting if you can access the same information on your laptop.

In the last thirty years, more and more devices have crept into our lives. For me, the process started with my first laptop well over a decade ago. Later I bought a dumb feature phone and then an even more distracting smartphone. Next came an iPad and a fitness tracker. I'm sure there will be more devices in my future.

This speaks to a trap we increasingly face: bringing new devices into our lives without first questioning their value. Clayton Christensen, a professor at Harvard Business School, developed a useful way of assessing the devices in your life: question what "jobs" you "hire" devices to do for you. Every product we buy should do a job for us—we hire Kleenex to blow our nose; Uber to get from one place to another; OpenTable to book a table at a restaurant; Match.com to find a partner.

We hire our phones to do a lot of these "jobs," maybe more than any other product we own. We hire them to be an alarm clock, camera, timepiece, GPS navigator, video game console, email and messaging machine, boarding pass, music player, radio, subway pass, datebook, map, and so much more. It's no wonder we spend so much time on them.

As we accumulate more devices, their jobs can become redundant. The only reason I have a tablet today is because I hire it as my distractions device. If I didn't need that particular service, it's likely I would have hired the tablet to do the exact same job done by my phone and computer—helping me surf the web and using social media—and it would have been totally unnecessary.

I recently got rid of my fitness tracker for this very reason—while it was a lot of fun at first, I couldn't remember what job I'd hired it to do. Several years back, I got rid of my TV and cable subscription for a similar reason: Netflix became my hire of choice for passive entertainment.

Before you buy another device, ask yourself: What jobs am I hiring it to do that the devices I already own can't? Thinking about your devices this way forces you to consider why you really own them and, perhaps even more important, enables you to bring devices into your life only with intention.

Email

In the knowledge economy, email is one of the largest distractions we face every day—it's usually the largest pain point for the people I speak to and coach (with meetings being a close second).

One of the best strategies to tame email is to limit how many email notifications you receive, which limits how frequently you're interrupted. Sixty-four percent of people use notifications with either audible or visual signals to alert them to new messages—if you fall into this category, you're probably spending too much time and attention on email.

In addition to limiting new message alerts, here are ten of my favorite email tactics. These will help you check your email more deliberately, and constrain how much time and attention you spend on it in the first place. Many of these strategies also work for other messaging apps, such as Slack.

- **Check for new messages only if you have the time, attention, and energy to deal with whatever might have come in.** This is a simple trigger that lets you make sure you can actually deal with new messages, instead of getting stressed by the new stuff to which you have to respond.

- **Keep a tally of how often you check for messages.** The average knowledge worker checks his email eleven times *per hour*—eighty-eight times over the span of a day. It's hard to get any real work done with so many interruptions. The same study found that employees spend an average of just around thirty-five minutes on email per day—which means that email consumes much more attention than it does actual time. Once you become aware of how often you check for new messages, you'll likely want to reduce that amount of time because of the high cost of interruptions.

- **Predecide when you'll check.** Determining ahead of time when you'll check for new messages works wonders for reducing the number of times you open your email. Seventy percent of emails are opened within the first six seconds of receipt, so shutting off notifications will help you work in a less agitated and reflexive way. I personally check new messages once a day at 3:00 p.m. and have an autoresponse that notifies people of this. If this frequency is unrealistic for your work, come up with a compatible number—as long as it's less than eighty-eight times over the span of a workday, you'll be doing better than average. It helps to schedule these blocks of time on your calendar and set an autoresponse, both to make you feel more comfortable and to hold you socially accountable. If you still find email too tempting, enable a distraction blocker to cut yourself off. Eighty-four percent of workers keep their email client open in the background as they work, but closing it will help you focus beyond the forty-second mark.

- **Hyperfocus on email.** If you work in an environment that demands that you be highly responsive to emails, try hyperfocusing while answering your messages. Set a timer for twenty minutes, and in that time, blow through as many emails as you possibly can. Even if you receive an extraordinary number of messages, hyperfocusing on your inbox for twenty minutes, even as often as at the top of each hour, will enable you to get back to people quickly and allow you to still accomplish meaningful work the rest of the time. Plus, at most, the senders will have to wait only forty to sixty minutes for a response.

- **Limit points of contact.** It takes only ten seconds to carry out one of the most important productivity tactics: deleting the email app

on your phone. I have an email app only on my distractions device
and on my computer.

- **Keep an external to-do list.** Your email application is the worst
possible place to keep a to-do list—it's distracting and overwhelming, and new stuff is constantly popping up, which makes it difficult to prioritize tasks and tell what's truly important. A task
list—where you simply keep a tally of what you have to get done
today, preferably with your three daily intentions at the top—is
simpler and much more powerful. While it takes an extra step to
move your actionable emails to a separate list, doing so will leave
you feeling much less overwhelmed and will enable you to better
organize what's on your plate.

- **Sign up for two email accounts.** I have two email addresses: one
that's public facing, and a private one for my closest colleagues.
While I check my public facing account once a day, I batch-check
the other inbox a few times throughout the day. In select cases, this
is a strategy worth adopting.

- **Take an "email holiday."** If you're hunkering down on a big project,
set up an autoresponder explaining that you're on a one- or two-day
"email holiday" and that you're still in the office and can be reached
by phone or in person for urgent requests. People are far more understanding of this strategy than you may think.

- **Use the five-sentence rule.** In order to save your time and respect
your email recipient's time, keep each message you write to five
sentences or less, and add a note to your email signature explaining
that you're doing so. If you feel the urge to write anything longer,

use that as an opportunity to pick up the phone. This may save you from engaging in an unnecessarily protracted email exchange.

- **Wait before sending important messages.** Not every email is worth sending immediately—this is particularly true when you find yourself in an emotionally charged state when drafting a reply. Some responses, you might ultimately decide, aren't worth sending at all. For important messages, heated exchanges, or emails that require more thought, give yourself time to respond—and let your mind wander to let new, better, and more creative ideas rise to the surface.

However we deal with it, email remains one of the most stressful elements of our work. One study that had participants go without email observed that after a period of just *one week*, their heart-rate variability changed as they became significantly less stressed. The subjects interacted more often with people, spent longer working on tasks, multitasked less, and became much more focused. The absence of email allowed people to work slowly and more deliberately. When the experiment ended, participants described the experience as liberating, peaceful, and refreshing. While it would be impossible to get rid of email completely, try the tactics above and experiment with what works best for you.

Meetings

After email, meetings are one of the biggest distractions we face throughout the day. They also consume an inordinate amount of time. A recent study found that, on average, knowledge workers spend 37 percent of their time in meetings—which means that if you work an eight-hour day, you typically spend three hours daily in meetings.

Meetings are remarkably costly—gather even a small group of

people in a conference room for an hour, and you can easily lose an entire day's worth of work. That's not counting the time it takes everyone to switch his or her attention to and from what's being discussed. There's nothing inherently wrong with such gatherings, but pointless meetings are one of the largest productivity drains in the modern office.

Here are four of my favorite ways to reel in the number of meetings you attend and make the ones you do take part in more productive:

- **Never attend a meeting without an agenda.** *Ever.* A meeting without an agenda is a meeting without a purpose. Whenever I'm invited to a meeting without an agenda, regardless of whom it's with, I'll ask for the objective. Very frequently, whoever scheduled it will find that the purpose can be accomplished with a couple of emails or a phone call. Push back on any meeting without an agenda— your time is too valuable.

- **Question every recurring meeting on your calendar.** We often fail to question the value of routine meetings. Sift through the next month or two on your calendar, and consider which recurring meetings are truly worth your time and attention. Some may be more valuable than they seem on the surface, especially when they enable you to connect and learn more about what your team is doing, but just as many aren't. Some may be difficult to get out of, but taking a few minutes to gracefully ease your way out will save *hours* later on.

- **Challenge the attendance list.** Does everybody invited need to be there? The answer is usually no. If you're a manager or team leader, or just want to save someone time, let certain participants whose presence isn't critical know that while they're definitely welcome, their attendance is optional if they have something else important to work on.

- **Hyperfocus on meetings.** Engaging can be tough when meetings consume more of your time than they do your attention and energy. But if you do decide a meeting is worth attending, or you can't get out of it, enjoy it! Leave your phone or your computer behind and focus on what everyone is saying, contribute what you can, and whenever you can, help move things along so that everyone can leave early. You may end up getting a lot of value out of the meeting after all.

Some of the best productivity strategies you'll adopt will seem obvious in hindsight, and I'd include the above suggestions in that category—each of them is a matter of common sense. However, the great benefit of any productivity book (though, granted, I'm a bit biased) is that it allows you to step back from your work to notice what you could be doing differently. As the saying goes, common sense isn't always common action.

The Internet

Quite a few of the distractions I've discussed in this section have something in common: they stem from the internet. As powerful a tool as the internet is, it distracts and interrupts us and can lead us to spend a lot of time on autopilot mode. Just as our mind wanders while we work, we often surf the internet in active daydreaming mode, switching among websites and apps without intention.

While reducing distractions and creating a distraction-free mode will go a long way toward helping you work with more intention, it's often worth taking this even a step further and disconnecting from the internet *entirely*. This can be beneficial not only at work. Being disconnected from the internet for a twelve-hour period at home is nothing short of refreshing. When you're traveling, you'll never be so productive and invigorated as after you decide not to buy access to the internet on a bus or a plane. You spend about half of your online time procrastinating—the benefits of being connected often simply aren't worth how much longer everything takes.

Don't just take my word for it: try disconnecting completely for a period of twenty-four hours this Sunday, and encourage your family to do the same. Instead of ponying up for internet access on the plane the next time you travel, work on an offline project that is important but not urgent. Reflect afterward: How restored do you feel? How much were you able to accomplish? If you're anything like me, you'll probably be motivated to limit your access to the internet in the future too.

SIMPLIFYING YOUR ENVIRONMENT

Several years ago I worked in the recruitment department of a large company. One of my coworkers, Penny, kept a small bowl of jelly beans on her desk. This in and of itself wasn't remarkable—but what I did find remarkable was the fact that *she ate almost none of them*. It's not that she didn't like jelly beans—she just wasn't tempted that much by food. Each day she'd nibble at a few, leaving the rest for anyone who happened to stop by.

I probably ate 90 percent of those jelly beans. Every time I walked by Penny's office, I'd grab a small handful of candy—an amount that was always, at least in my eyes, asymptotically close to the socially acceptable limit. If I had a similar bowl in my office, I don't think it would have lasted the afternoon. (This past Friday, my fiancée and I hosted a party, and we had two bags of chips left over. I ate both within two days.)

My friends are often surprised when I share stories like this—as someone who researches and experiments with productivity as a full-time job, I'm pretty sure some of them expect me to have a superhuman level of self-control. But much as I do to resist digital distractions when writing, I try to deal with other temptations in my life ahead of time. Because food is my biggest weakness, I modify my external environment to avoid keeping any unhealthy snacks in the house, and if they are around, I ask someone to hide them.

Whether with food or distractions, we're highly influenced by our external environment. Takeout menus stuck on your refrigerator are a reminder that tasty, unhealthy food is only a call away—just as keeping cut-up vegetables and hummus in the fridge will remind you to eat healthier. Posting your three daily intentions in a visible place will remind you to work on what's actually important throughout the day. Keeping a TV in your bedroom will remind you that a world of news and entertainment can be accessed with just the press of a button—an object of attention much more enticing than sleep. Facing your couches and chairs toward the TV, instead of toward one another, will have a similarly tempting effect. Leaving your phone on the table when eating breakfast will introduce an environmental cue that reminds you a world of distraction awaits.*

External environmental cues can affect us in remarkable ways. One study observed coffee shop patrons conversing with one another and discovered that those who kept their phone in front of them checked it every three to five minutes, "regardless of whether it rang or buzzed." As the study put it, "Even when they are not in active use or buzzing, beeping, ringing, or flashing, [our phones] are representative of [our] wider social network and a portal to an immense compendium of information." Another study concluded, somewhat sadly, that the "mere presence of a cell phone placed innocuously in the visual field of

---

* This is the irony of using our smartphone when we're socializing with another person. We largely use the device to cultivate relationships with other people, but no smartphone experience will ever be as meaningful as a face-to-face encounter.

participants was found to interfere with closeness, connection, and re-lationship quality."

So often these cues in our environment pull us away from what we intend to accomplish—and, on a personal level, make our experiences less meaningful. Environmental cues don't actively interrupt us, like notifications, but they can do just as much harm to our productivity and personal life. This is especially the case when we look around for a novel distraction from a complex task. Our working environment should hold as few of these distracting cues as possible. When we keep our phone, tablet, and television in another room, we are derailed less often, become accustomed to working in a less stimulating environ-ment, and ensure the environment around us is not more attractive than what we intend to focus on.

By eliminating the novel cues in our working environment, we give ourselves the ability to focus for much longer. It's worth becoming de-liberate about the cues you allow into your environment and question-ing how they might affect your productivity.*

Since observing how much time and attention I waste on devices like my tablet and smartphone, I've rarely kept them in my external environment, unless they serve a purpose. My tablet is currently in another room, and my phone is on a table across my office, well out of

---

* Environmental cues are powerful—even the cleanliness of your office has an impact on your productivity. Research shows that neat environments are more conducive to focus, and messy environments are more conducive to creativity. For this reason, if you want all the participants in a meeting to focus on a project, invite them into a clean conference room with few distractions. If you want to break with convention, effect change, or have a more creative brainstorming session, hold the meeting in a messier environment. If there isn't a cluttered meeting room at the office, mix things up and have a meeting off-site, such as outdoors in nature, where everyone is exposed to new insight triggers. (Though be wary of walking meetings. Walking—including while you work, such as on a treadmill desk—has been shown to decrease cognitive performance. Performance increases *after* a walk, however.)

reach.* There's a lot of stuff in front of me: a meditation cushion, a pair of adjustable dumbbells, several plants, a cup of matcha tea, pictures of family, a fidget cube, a whiteboard, and my turtle, Edward, basking on her† rock. These things won't derail my attention for long—they simply aren't that complex—so, unlike a smartphone, they can't completely hijack my attention. If I do get distracted by them, it's much easier to notice that my mind has wandered, and it's easier for me to get back on track.

Novel objects of attention threaten to invade your attentional space and prevent you from focusing completely on any one thing.

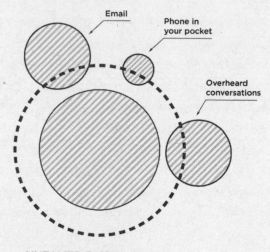

UNTAMED DISTRACTIONS

---

* One study found that when a distraction is about twenty seconds away from us—when it takes twenty seconds to retrieve a bag of chips from the basement, unlock a drawer to get our cellphone, or restart our computer to access distracting websites—it provides enough of a temporal distance for us to not fall victim to these distractions, and we're better able to control our impulses. It's in this space between impulse and action that we regain control over our attention—and introducing a twenty-second delay gives us the awareness to resist the impulses we naturally have.

† Long story . . .

To modify your environment to be more conducive to working or living, you should eliminate objects of attention that will potentially derail your focus.

Doing this is actually pretty simple:

1. **Take stock of the distractions around you.** This is especially important in the place where you focus on your most complex work. Make a list of all potential distractions—everything from the tablet you keep by your desk to a coworker sharing your cubicle. Then consider: Which of these do you find more attractive than your work?

2. **Distance yourself.** Just as with distractions, it's not possible to tame all environmental cues in advance—but you can control most. Make a plan to remove attractive objects of attention from your environment so you're not tempted by them.

3. **Introduce more productive cues into your environment.** Not all environmental cues are bad, and no one wants to work in a sterile environment. Plants, for example, have been shown to have a calming effect—we evolved to feel good in nature, not in cubicles. Hanging a whiteboard in your environment may prompt you to brainstorm your thoughts and is a useful place to write your three daily intentions. Lining up your favorite books on an office shelf might remind you of ideas as you work. Keeping a fidget cube by your side is a cue to occasionally take a break, daydream, and consider new ideas. Having a book on your nightstand, instead of your phone, will encourage you to read more. Storing your fruit in a bowl on the table, instead of in your refrigerator, will prompt you to eat healthier.

The cleanliness of your environment is also important. Make sure you tidy your space when you're done with it—coming home to a mess of dishes in the sink and random objects strewn all over the floor will instantly stress you out, reminding you of all the things you still have to do. The same applies when you finish working for the day: tidy the papers on your desk, close the windows on your computer, sort files on your desktop, and act on and archive each email you received that day. When you sit down at your desk the next morning, you'll be able to focus immediately on your intentions, instead of becoming stressed about the previous day's progress. Decluttering your digital environment is just as important as decluttering your physical one.

If you ask people in what places they're most productive, few will answer "The office." In fact, most people will name any place *but* the office—including their favorite coffee shop, an airport, the train, or their home office. The reason for this, I'd argue, is that these environments contain fewer cues for all we have to get done: we don't overhear coworkers chatting about the projects we're working on; we don't walk by the meeting rooms where we regularly share progress reports. Mixing up where we work often lets us focus on what we intend to accomplish, without distracting cues.

As you've probably found, environmental cues can also help our future selves. After I set my three overarching intentions for the following day at the end of the day prior, I write them on my whiteboard so they're what I see first thing in the morning. If I need to remember to bring a few documents to a meeting, I'll put them by the door so I see them as I leave.

MUSIC

There are an awful lot of factors in the environment that affect focus—even office temperature influences productivity to some degree.* Before getting to how your internal, mental environment influences your productivity, I want to zero in on one more external factor. It may be something you work with already: music.

While researching *Hyperfocus*, I interviewed one of the most renowned musicians of our time, one who has sold more music than Prince, Britney Spears, Justin Bieber, or Bob Dylan. The man has almost single-handedly crafted the soundtrack to countless childhoods, and his videos easily attract millions of YouTube views.

However, while you may recognize his music, you likely won't know Jerry Martin's name. Jerry composed the music scores for video games such as *The Sims* and *SimCity*—games that have collectively sold well over 100 million copies worldwide. He's also created soundtracks for Apple, General Motors, and NBA commercials. Jerry's music is the perfect place to start when looking at how music influences productivity, as he has created some of the most productive soundtracks in existence.

Research suggests that the most productive music has two main attributes: it sounds familiar (because of this, music that is productive for you may differ from your coworkers' choices), and it's relatively simple. Jerry's music hits both of these notes. It sounds comfortably familiar, since it's heavily influenced by famous composers like George Gershwin. It contains no words to distract you, and it's simple. As Martin told me, "When you put too much structure in music, you tend to focus on it. The best kind of music exists in the background—there's really not much going on when you listen closely. The music is linear, changing without you knowing it, and is supporting your work in the

---

* One study found that 70–72°F (21–22°C) is the ideal temperature for productivity. Lower temperatures increase the number of errors we make and how often we call in sick, and higher temperatures, above 86°F (30°C), decrease our productivity by about 10 percent. We're all wired differently, of course, so your mileage may vary.

game." For my own part, I love writing to songs on repeat and have been listening to the same depressing Ed Sheeran tune for the last hour.

However, research also suggests that the most productive music is *relative*. Music occupies at least some portion of attentional space—but it occupies less when it's familiar, simple, and also relatively quiet. As a result, music is no competition for a quiet environment when it comes to focus, but of course, music never exists in isolation.

If you're working in a busy coffee shop, music may help obscure the conversations around you, which are much more complex and distracting than a simple and familiar melody. If a loud coworker in the adjacent cubicle is on a telephone call, it's much more productive to throw on some noise-canceling headphones and listen to music. (A study found that overhearing one side of a phone conversation is significantly more distracting than overhearing a regular dyadic conversation—your brain works overtime to fill in the missing side of the half-alogue, so the conversation occupies more of your attentional space.)* For me, the quiet serenity offered by music on noise-canceling headphones on a loud flight is much less distracting than the roar of the plane's engine. When I'm at a coffee shop and they inexplicably switch the soundtrack to talk radio, I'll listen to music.

Your own experience with how music affects your productivity will vary depending on the nature of your work, your working environment, and even your personality—music impairs the performance of introverts

---

* Secondhand distraction is a real phenomenon: another experiment found that students who focused on a lecture were likely to score significantly worse if they could see a classmate multitasking on a laptop in front of them—these distracted students averaged 56 percent on a follow-up test, while those who weren't distracted scored 73 percent. That can be the equivalent of going from a D to a B grade. For this reason, some researchers advocate developing an "attention-aware classroom" in which students can be mindful of the cost of distractions. On the flip side, excessive classroom computer use can also be symptomatic of a larger problem—like that the lecture is boring and students aren't engaged.

more than extroverts, for example. However, generally speaking, if you're looking to focus, keep the music you listen to simple and familiar.

CLEARING YOUR MIND

Of course, not all distractions are external, as we also keep a lot of distracting stuff in our heads. When writing a report, we remember we had a meeting that started ten minutes ago; when we arrive home from work, we realize we forgot to stop to pick up bread. Clearing our head of these "open loops" is critical so they don't distract us in the moment as we're trying to focus.

It's impossible to write about focus and productivity without citing David Allen's work. Allen is the author of *Getting Things Done*, a book with a simple premise: that our brain is for *having* ideas, not for holding them. An empty brain is a productive brain, and the more stuff we get out of our heads, the more clearly we think.

You're already familiar with this idea if you keep a calendar. You'd never be able to think clearly if you tried to keep track of all of your appointments and meetings in your head. You'd forever need to devote some portion of your attentional space to upcoming events, and this would be extraordinarily stressful. Keeping a to-do list has a similar effect: each task you get out of your head and onto the list is a task that won't pester you as you're working on something else. You'll be able to think more clearly—and you'll experience less guilt about what you're working on as a result.

Something remarkable happens when you externalize tasks and commitments: you work with almost no guilt, worry, or doubt. You experience guilt when you feel tension about your past; worry when you feel tension about your future; and doubt and stress when you feel tension about the present moment. These feelings evaporate when you set intentions and make a rough plan for how you'll complete your important tasks. You'll think more clearly too—externalizing what's on your mind means tasks and commitments won't pop into your attentional space as you're working.

Maintaining a calendar or a to-do list turns internal distractions into external cues. You no longer need to keep in mind that you have a meeting—your calendar app will do that for you. You don't need to remember to work on what's important—the task list on your desk acts as a cue to remind you of what you need to get done, especially when you keep your most important daily intentions at the top.

This concept extends far beyond your tasks and appointments. Keeping a distractions list as you focus will remove distractions from your head so you can refocus more quickly and deal with them later (see chapter 0.5). If you're a worrier, create a list of everything weighing on your mind (while scheduling a time to consider the validity of each of the entries). Capturing ideas that come to you as you let your mind rest and wander will mean you can make use of them later. Regularly reviewing a list of everything you're waiting for—one that records the important emails, letters, packages, and phone calls you're expecting— will get these things off your mind, too.

Some people can get by with the bare minimum—keeping a to-do list and a calendar—and find additional lists cumbersome. Others find they think most clearly when they capture every little thing weighing on their minds. I personally fall somewhere in between. Feel out your own threshold: start with setting a few intentions each day, and keep a to-do list and a calendar. Unresolved mental loops can tug at your attention throughout the day, especially when you're immersed in your most important work. Begin closing these open loops so you can focus, and hyperfocus, more easily on your work.

Continuously capture unresolved commitments and ideas as they come up, and get into a habit of revisiting them at a set time later. This will free up a lot of attentional space to spend on better things.

WORKING WITH PURPOSE

Here is a fundamental truth about focus: your brain will invariably resist more complex tasks, especially when you're first starting them—and when it does, you'll look around for more novel and stimulating things to do instead. When you clear your working environment of interruptions, distractions, and cues that will tempt you away from what you intend to accomplish in the moment, you'll stay on track. This chapter was long for a simple reason: there's a lot of brush you need to clear before you can hyperfocus.

Recall the three measures we can use to measure the quality of our attention: how much time we spend working with intention; how long we're able to focus on one task; and how long our mind wanders before we catch it doing so.

All three measures are supported by the tactics in this chapter:

- Creating a distraction-free mode lets you carve out time to spend intentionally while eliminating the more attractive objects of attention that would ordinarily derail your focus.
- Working with fewer distractions in general lets you eliminate novel objects of attention throughout the day and reclaim more of your attention for what's important.
- Utilizing both of these working modes helps you train your brain to wander less and focus longer.
- Simplifying your working and living environments eliminates a slew of tempting distractions.
- Clearing your head of distracting open loops lets you work more clearly and frees even more attentional space for your most productive tasks.

One final benefit of eliminating distractions in advance is gaining the freedom to work at a slower, more purposeful pace. One study, for example, found that when we text while reading something, it can take us anywhere from 22 percent to 59 percent longer to read the same passage. It doesn't matter if you work at a slower, more deliberate pace if you're continuously working in the right direction. What you lose in speed you make up for in intentionality.

Carving out more attentional space for what you're doing also enables you to work with greater awareness—of what distractions you're resisting, how you feel about your work, how much energy you have, and whether you need to recharge. In addition, you will actually notice temptations and impulses that arise, so you'll fall victim to them less often in the future.

So far we've covered the four stages of hyperfocus: choosing an object of attention, eliminating distractions, focusing on a task, and getting back on track.

Now let's talk about how you can make a habit out of setting the stage for this superproductive state of mind by increasing the size of your attentional space and overcoming your resistance to hyperfocus.

MAKING HYPERFOCUS A HABIT

CHAPTER 5

WHAT MAKES OUR MINDS WANDER

There is a wealth of research that examines why our mind wanders at the exact time we're trying to focus. It does so significantly more when

- we're feeling stressed or bored;
- we're working in a chaotic environment;
- we're dealing with and thinking about a number of personal concerns;
- we're questioning whether we're working on the most productive or meaningful task; or
- we have unused attentional space—the more we have, the more prone we are to mind-wandering episodes.

Conveniently, we've already discussed these factors:

- **Feeling stressed or bored:** We experience stress when the demands of a situation exceed our ability to cope with them. By preventing

attentional space overload, we ensure we have the resources needed
to cope with such conditions.

- **Working in a chaotic environment**: I define boredom as the restlessness we feel as we transition from a state of high stimulation to
a lower one. In becoming accustomed to experiencing less stimulation over time—by enabling our distraction-free mode whenever we
hyperfocus, and by working with fewer distractions in general—we
face this stimulation gap less often, experience boredom less frequently, and make our environment less chaotic by default.

- **Thinking about personal concerns**: Capturing our mind's "open
loops"—through a task list, a waiting-for list, or even a worry list—
prevents unresolved items from weighing on our mind as we try to
focus. This helps us deal better with chaotic environments and set
aside personal concerns. Switching tasks less frequently also helps us
think more clearly—we experience less attentional residue, which
can take a toll on our limited attentional space.

- **Questioning whether we're working on the best thing**: Working
with intention is the best way to experience fewer feelings of doubt
about what we should or could be doing in any one moment.
These feelings lead our minds to wander from what we're trying to
focus on.

- **Amount of unused attentional space**: Deploying hyperfocus to
work on our most complex tasks will consume more attentional
space by default, which will in turn prevent our mind from wandering. The smaller the object of attention, the more likely mental
wandering will occur.

The tactics in this book work for a few main reasons: while they all enable you to focus more deeply, they also safeguard your mind from wandering in the first place. Later in the book we'll examine a few other factors that lead your mind to wander, including how tired you are and how happy you feel. (Your happiness level can impact your attention in many curious ways.)

For now, though, let's dive deeper into the mind-wandering factor I personally find most interesting: the attentional space we have to spare.

THE POWER OF MAKING YOUR WORK HARDER

Depending on their complexity, tasks will require varying amounts of your attentional space. If you've ever tried to meditate and focus only on your breath for a few minutes, you might have noticed your mind wanders more than usual—far more than when you're going for a run, carrying on a deep conversation, or watching a movie. These latter tasks are more complex and fill more of your attentional space by default.*

Consciously making your tasks more complex, and taking on more complex ones, is another powerful way to enter into a hyperfocused state, as they will consume more of your attention. This will keep you more engaged in what you're doing and lead your mind to wander less often.

In his groundbreaking book *Flow*, Mihaly Csikszentmihalyi offers intriguing insights about when we're most likely to enter into a flow state: when the challenge of completing a task is roughly equal to our

---

* The power of meditation is that reining your mind to focus on a small and simple object of attention makes focusing on more complex things easier. As a result, your mind wanders less often, you're able to focus more deeply and for longer periods, and the quality of your attention increases dramatically. Meditation practices are less intimidating than you may think and are worth trying.

ability to do so, and we become totally immersed in the task. When our skills greatly exceed the demands of a task—such as when we do mindless data entry for several hours—we feel bored. When the demands of a task exceed our skills—such as when we're unprepared to give a presentation—we feel anxious. When the demands of a task are roughly equal to our ability to do that task—when we're playing an instrument, immersed in a book, or skiing down a freshly powdered slope—we're a lot more likely to be fully engaged in what we're doing.

If you find it difficult to become immersed in your work throughout the day, it's worth questioning whether your tasks are difficult and complex enough. If you're frequently bored, consider whether your job takes advantage of your unique skill set. If your mind is still frequently wandering, even after implementing the ideas in the previous chapters, it's a pretty good sign your tasks aren't complex enough and don't consume enough of your attentional space.* On the opposite end of the spectrum, if you find you're anxious at work even *after* taming distractions and working with more intention, consider whether your current skills are a good match for the tasks at hand.

Outside of questioning individual tasks, it's also worth reflecting on how challenging you find your workload *in general*. The tactics in *Hyperfocus* will allow you to accomplish more in less time, but you may then find you don't have enough work remaining to fill that extra time. This can manifest itself in some odd ways.

Our work tends to expand to fit the available completion time—in productivity circles, this phenomenon is known as Parkinson's law. But by disabling distractions in advance, you may find the same thing I did: your work no longer expands to fit the time you have available for

---

* The larger your attentional space, the more your mind wanders when you work on something simple. This is further evidence that the smartest members of your team should be assigned the most challenging work.

its completion, and you discover how much work you truly have on your plate. Some executives I coach find they're able to accomplish a full day's work in just a few hours when they focus on only their most consequential tasks.

I discovered this phenomenon firsthand with my last book. After handing in the eighty-thousand-word manuscript, which I wrote in a relatively short amount of time, I continued to be just as busy—even though I had substantially less work. My remaining projects expanded to fit the time I had available. Instead of planning for speaking engagements a few weeks before they were scheduled, I began to think about them much further in advance, far earlier than I needed to. I logged into my social media accounts more often, when I should have been working. I stopped following my own advice and checked for new emails constantly instead of once a day. I enabled more notifications and alerts so I would have more tasks to tend to. And I agreed to more meetings, many of which I didn't need to attend in the first place. I experienced a dreaded feeling of guilt whenever I wasn't busy, which, of course, disappeared as soon as I did more busywork.

Little did I know that this guilt had two sources: a lack of working with intent and my work expanding to fill how much time I had for it. It took several months before I finally stepped back to tame the novel distractions that were flooding my available time. In doing so I discovered how little work I actually had on my plate. In response I intentionally took on more meaningful tasks—writing more for my website, thinking about this book, and ramping up my speaking and coaching sessions. Because I think of myself as a pretty productive guy, my failure was tough to admit to myself, but it taught me an essential lesson: doing mindless stuff at work or at home is not only unproductive but also a sign you don't have enough important work. This also accounts for why busywork gets set aside when you're on deadline: there's no time available to contain its expansion.

To measure if you have enough work in general, assess how much of your day you spend doing unproductive busywork. If you're high on the busywork scale, you may have room to take on significantly more tasks—and become more engaged and productive in the process.

This advice is counterintuitive, and the very idea may turn you off if you already feel you're working at capacity. But it's worth considering. When we do knowledge work for a living, we procrastinate, spending time and attention on email and social media, tasks that make us *feel* productive in our work but lead us to accomplish little.

A note on rote tasks. While rote work is often less productive than complex tasks, it is redeeming in one way: it's usually more *fun*. Studies show we prefer mundane tasks like data entry over more complex tasks like writing reports. In writing this book, I visited Microsoft's research department, which conducts many studies on how we manage our attention. On each of my three trips there, the staff was adamant in confirming that we're happier doing tasks that don't consume our complete attention. This makes sense: while our productive tasks are important, they're usually also more aversive, which is why we're usually well compensated to do them—they take advantage of our unique mental resources. At the same time, mindless work can give us immediate feedback and the sense of having accomplished something. If certain rote tasks bring you genuine enjoyment, don't let a productivity book make you stop doing them. But do eliminate some to carve out more time and attention for significant tasks.

INCREASING THE SIZE OF YOUR
ATTENTIONAL SPACE

Most of the focus strategies I've discussed so far involve becoming a better custodian of your attentional space. In addition to more deliberately managing it, you can also increase its size.

To recap, the size of attentional space is determined by a measure that cognitive psychology refers to as "working memory capacity"—how many pieces of data you can hold in your mind simultaneously (usually about four chunks of information). The greater your working memory capacity, the more information you can hold at the same time and the greater your ability to process complex tasks.

As well as allowing you to take on more complex tasks, expanding your attentional space offers other benefits. A higher working memory capacity has been shown to reduce mind wandering when you're focused on complex tasks. When your mind does wander, it actually wanders more productively—the larger the size of your attentional space, the more likely you are to think about (and plan for) the future. Even better, a larger attentional space means you'll have extra attention to think about what you'll work on next, while keeping your original intention in mind. A larger attentional space also helps you get back on track quicker after your mind wanders or you become distracted. One study expressed this memorably when it stated that possessing a greater working memory capacity "enables [you] to take full advantage of these underutilized resources and return to [your] favored mental destination."*

So how exactly *do* you expand the size of your attentional space?

There are many "brain training" apps and websites that promise to

---

* There is a strong relationship between working memory capacity and intelligence—an 85 percent correlation. Intelligence is the single best predictor of job performance.

build memory and attention. Simply put, most of their claims are dubious—in laboratory studies, they simply don't hold water. While a few brain-training programs work in the short term and help you remember a bit more and problem-solve a bit better, their impact ends there. You have to stick with them for several hours a week in order for them to continue working, and as soon as you stop, you lose the gains you've made. One study measured the effectiveness of these programs across a sample size of 11,430 participants. It found "no evidence" that the apps worked, even when the tasks they measured were the ones they were designed to improve!

There is, however, one practice that has been proven in study after study to increase working memory capacity: meditation.

Meditation gets a bad rap and often conjures images of a monk meditating in a cave. In practice it's actually quite simple. Like hyperfocus, meditation involves continually returning your focus to a single object of attention—usually your breath—as soon as you notice your mind has wandered from it.

In breathing meditation (the most common form, and the one I've personally practiced for about a decade), you notice the characteristics of your breath: how deeply it ebbs and flows, its temperature, where it is most prominent in your body, how your in-breath transitions to your out-breath, and so on. Since observing your breath doesn't consume your full attention, your mind will wander *constantly*—which is somewhat the point. Each time you return your wandering mind to the details of your breath, you heighten your executive functioning: how much control you have over your attention. This eventually enables you to improve each measure of the quality of your attention. You'll be able to focus for longer, your mind will wander less, and you'll be able to work with greater intention.

You experience this same benefit during hyperfocus. Like meditation, hyperfocus is a practice that compounds upon itself—the more you practice, the more you learn to manage your attention and the longer you're able to focus the next time around.

Meditation is simple—sit somewhere with your eyes closed and pay attention to your breath. It's natural to feel as if you're doing it wrong, especially at first, but don't overthink it. The effects of this simple practice are actually profound. One study discovered that when participants developed a meditation practice, not only did their minds wander less, but they could also focus for longer before that happened— two measures of the quality of attention. This study introduced meditation to students studying for the GRE—a standardized graduate admissions test in the United States. When it came time for them to take the test, their scores rose an average of *16 percent*! Meditation has also been shown to prevent "the deterioration of [working memory capacity] during periods of high stress"—such as working in a chaotic environment or dealing with personal concerns. One review of the literature on the subject described meditation's benefits most succinctly, calling it "the most validated technique for minimizing the disruptive effects of mind wandering."

My favorite study of meditation measured how much participants' working memory capacity increased when they had an active meditation practice. The researchers guided participants through a forty-five-minute meditation exercise twice a week and encouraged them to meditate at home. A few weeks later they discovered something incredible in the working memory capacity of everyone who meditated: it increased by an average of *more than 30 percent*. That was significantly more than that of two other groups of subjects in the study, one of which practiced yoga for several weeks. This effect was also observed after a period of just a few weeks.

To begin meditating requires just a few minutes each day. Start by determining your resistance level, as you do before hyperfocusing on a task. Then sit in a chair, in a comfortable but upright posture so the

disks of your spine are stacked one on top of another. Notice the qual-
ities of your breath and refocus on them whenever your mind wanders.
I highly recommend using an app to get started—I like Headspace and
Insight Timer, which both feature guided meditations to help you get
started. Approach each meditation session with a genuine curiosity
about where your mind will wander. My meditation rule is simple, and
one I've stuck with for years: it doesn't matter how long I meditate, as
long as I do so each day. Some days I can spare only a minute or two,
which is sufficient as long as I keep faithful to a routine. When I began
a decade ago, I did only five-minute sessions, and since then have
slowly built to thirty minutes. I wouldn't give it up for anything.

When you practice being with your breath, you practice being with
your life. But meditation is not the only tool in this tool kit. Practicing
mindfulness is another proven way to increase the size of your attentional space. It's similar to meditation but a little less intimidating.

Mindfulness is about becoming conscious of what is filling your
mind and noticing the circumstances of the current moment. This includes noting anything you happen to be perceiving, feeling, or thinking. Mindfulness differs from hyperfocus in one major respect: it's
about focusing on the circumstances of the present, rather than becoming immersed in them.

Here's a statement that might sound strange: you've never really
taken a shower. While you might stand there while the water washes
over you, your mind is usually elsewhere—at the office, running
through your daily checklist, thinking about what you need to buy for
dinner, or brainstorming about a problem you're facing at work. While
a small part of it runs through the habit sequence of taking a shower,
your mind isn't with you, present with what you're experiencing. A
mindful shower is one in which you focus on the sights, sounds, and
sensations of the present, which enables you to train your brain to better focus on what's in front of you.

Begin to practice mindfulness by choosing one daily task that doesn't consume your complete attention—sipping your morning coffee, walking through your office, or taking a shower—and intentionally be with that experience for a minute or two. Anchor your attention to the circumstances of the present moment—notice the smell, taste, and feeling of a cup of coffee; the momentum shifts in your body as you walk from one room in the office to another; or the temperature and sensations of taking a shower. You can set a timer or not—simply be with the circumstances of the present moment and notice as much as you can about what you're seeing, hearing, and feeling. When you find yourself becoming lost in thought, bring your mind back to what you originally intended to focus on—and laugh at how difficult it can be to tame. Don't be hard on yourself when your mind wanders—remember, your brain was built to do this.

Here's the key: the smaller the object of attention, the more your mind will wander, but the more you'll expand the size of your attentional space as you focus on it. The more quickly you're able to get back on track after your mind ventures off during a mindfulness or meditation session, the better you'll become at focusing at work and at home.

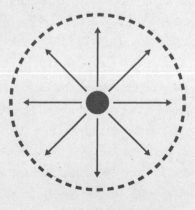

MEDITATION

Practices like meditation and mindfulness are also powerful because they train you to practice holding a single intention in your mind for a given period of time. During your meditation, you sit with the intention of being with your breath until your timer goes off. The same is true when you practice mindfulness: until the coffee cup is empty (or half full), your shower is finished, or you're done walking to where you intend to go, you focus on what you're doing then and there. When you keep a single intention in mind, you're able to live and work more intentionally for the rest of the day too. And because both meditation and mindfulness increase the size of your attentional space, both practices make you more likely to maintain intentions.

As if these benefits weren't enough, meditation and mindfulness also help you step back from your thoughts. This makes it infinitely easier to check what's occupying your attentional space. The more you notice what's grasped your attention, the more quickly you'll be able to redirect it to your intention. With enough awareness, you might even notice your mind has wandered to somewhere productive and you want to continue that train of thought. For example, a higher working memory capacity means your mind is more likely to make plans and set intentions for the future. With this extra awareness, you gain the power to notice stray objects of attention at the edges of your attentional space, such as when you're seeking external stimulation or about to fall victim to a seductive distraction.

The research is clear: mindfulness and meditation improve virtually every aspect of how you manage your attention.

Every once in a while, I like to travel to a local Buddhist monastery to join a public Saturday-afternoon meditation. This usually consists of a potluck and an hourlong meditation session, followed by a talk given by one of the monks. During one of my visits, a monk spoke about how for several weeks during his meditation practice he focused solely on the sensation his breath made on the tip of his nose—an impossibly small object of attention. I tried doing the same during an extended two-hour meditation practice the next day, and my mind has never wandered so much. With an object of attention that small, it's no surprise.

But the following Monday morning, I focused more deeply on my work than I had in weeks. I wrote several thousand words in just a few hours, brainstormed three talks, and had time left over to clear my email inboxes. The positive effects lingered beyond that day, as I was able to focus better throughout the week. The quality of attention is so integral to productivity that increasing it even slightly makes a remarkable difference in how much we accomplish.

Luckily, you don't have to spend hours focusing on the tip of your nose to experience the remarkable benefits of mindfulness and meditation. Even only a few minutes a day will help immensely. If you take away one lesson from this chapter, it should be that few practices will improve the quality of your attention—and the size of your attentional space—more than meditation and mindfulness. While both will consume some of your time, you'll make that time back, and then some, in how much more clearly, deeply, and deliberately you'll think and focus.

HYPERFOCUS AT HOME

Almost every idea in this book will help you not only at work but at home too. As I've put these ideas into practice, I've noticed some remarkable benefits in my personal life.

Chances are you were in hyperfocus mode during your last highly productive work period. You were likely in a similar state the last time you felt happiest and energized at home. You were probably focused on just one thing—whether that was carrying on a meaningful conversation with a loved one, planting a garden, playing cards with a relative, or relaxing with a book on the beach. The one thing you were doing consumed your full attentional space. Because of this, you likely didn't have many surrounding distractions—your work phone may have been in the other room, and you may have made a commitment to disconnect for the weekend. Your family may have agreed to a phone-free dinner. You were probably also in a more relaxed state and, because of this, didn't seek novel stimuli in your environment. You could focus with relative ease on what you were doing.

"Hyperfocus" was the best term I could come up with to describe this state of being totally focused on one thing, though it does have the disadvantage of sounding dauntingly intense. In practice, hyperfocus is actually quite relaxed, unless you're on a deadline or are working at or above capacity, so your work doesn't have the luxury of expanding to fit an amount of time. When you hyperfocus, you're surrounded by very few novel objects of attention, and what you're doing fills your attentional space quite naturally. This same idea holds true at home, and we experience the same benefits of hyperfocus there. We remember more of what we're doing, and our experiences become more meaningful as a result. We spend more time in the moment and get things done more quickly and with less effort. I like to do this by setting three personal daily intentions in addition to my three work goals, even if one happens to be binge-watching a show on Netflix.

One area I've noticed that particularly benefits from hyperfocus is conversations. The secret to deep, meaningful conversations is simple: bring your complete attention to the person you're speaking with. You can do this in many ways, such as by allowing someone to finish talking before you start (a simple but highly underutilized technique). Wait until you hear the period at the end of their sentence before you think about what you'll say next. I'm convinced that most people have a sixth sense and can tell when you're truly paying attention to them. It's a remarkable thing when you spend not just quality time with someone but quality attention as well.

Hyperfocus lets me dive deeper into my personal relationships, in conversation and other aspects. I'm convinced that love is nothing more than sharing quality attention with someone. As David Augsburger, a Baptist minister and author, has put it: "Being heard is so close to being loved that for the average person, they are almost indistinguishable."

When we're hyperfocusing on an activity at home—whether it's playing an instrument, walking the dog, or making dinner for the family—disabling the pointless, novel distractions and focusing completely on what we're doing means we are purposefully disengaging from our work. This practice gets easier with time. I've devoted an entire later chapter of this book to recharging hyperfocus—we can do this by periodically stepping back from our work to let our mind rest, wander, and take on less challenging tasks. Spending our time at home more purposefully also enables us to feel recharged.

Whether at work or at home, the quality of your attention determines the quality of your life. At work, the more attention you give to what's in front of you, the more productive you become. At home, the more attention you devote to what's in front of you, the more meaningful your life becomes.

FOUR (MORE) WAYS TO BATTLE
YOUR RESISTANCE TO HYPERFOCUS

This chapter covers a number of tactics that will help you develop an even stronger hyperfocus habit: making your work more challenging, taking on more projects at work and at home, increasing the size of your attentional space, practicing hyperfocus in all areas of life, and choosing exactly when to hyperfocus. Let's end with one final, important concept that will help you to solidify a hyperfocus ritual in your work and life: how to battle your inevitable resistance to the mode.

Assuming you've already given hyperfocus a try, even if only for ten minutes, you may have felt what I did at first: a mental resistance to focusing on just one thing. This was probably a mixture of restlessness, anxiousness, and succumbing to novel distractions. You likely found yourself craving these distractions more than usual in the initial stage of entering the hyperfocused state.

This resistance we feel toward complex and productive tasks isn't distributed evenly across working time—it's usually concentrated at the beginning of when we start these tasks:

40 s

For example, while it might take weeks to summon the energy and stamina needed to clean the garage or bedroom closet, once we do it for even just a minute, we could keep going for hours. The same is true for working out—after we overcome our resistance to getting started, we can go on with the rest of our workout. Starting provides enough momentum to carry out our intentions.

This is true of our most complex tasks as well, and is one of the many reasons we'll work on a task for only forty seconds before falling victim to distractions. We feel the most resistance at the very start and search instead for more attractive alternatives. When we begin a new task, working on it for at least one minute with purposeful attention and limited distractions is critical. Here are my four favorite strategies for battling this initial resistance:

1. **Shrink your desired hyperfocus period until you no longer feel resistance to the ritual.** Minimize the amount of time you'll dedicate to focusing on one task until you no longer feel mental resistance to it. Even setting a mental deadline of five minutes will likely be enough to get you started.

2. **Notice when you "don't have time" for something.** You always have time—you just spend it on other things. When you find yourself saying this familiar statement, try doing a task swap. For example: if you "don't have the time" to catch up with a friend over coffee, ask yourself whether you'd have an equal amount of time to watch the football game or surf Facebook. If you feel you "don't have time" to take something on, ask yourself whether you could free up your schedule enough to meet with your boss or clean your inbox. If the task swap shows you *do* have the time, chances are this is just your resistance talking.

3. **Continually practice hyperfocus.** Incorporate at least one hyperfocus interval each day. You'll experience less resistance as you get accustomed to working with fewer distractions and appreciate how productive you've become.

4. **Recharge!** Hyperfocus can be oddly energizing: you spend less energy regulating your behavior when you don't have to continually resist distractions and push yourself to focus on what's important. That said, resisting the ritual can also be a sign you need to recharge.

THE POWER OF HYPERFOCUS

Every idea in *Hyperfocus* is designed to help you more deliberately manage your attention—an essential idea when our attention is so limited and in demand.

Let's recap a few of these ideas:

- Understanding the four types of productive and unproductive work tasks lets us step back and figure out what's actually important so we can stop working on mindless autopilot mode.
- Recognizing the limits of our attention enables us to become aware of how few things we're able to focus on in the moment.
- Hyperfocusing on our most complex, productive tasks lets us activate the most productive mode of our brains and get a large amount accomplished in a short amount of time.
- Setting strong daily intentions lets us work on our most productive tasks.
- Creating a personalized distraction-free mode, and a reduced-distractions mode, lets us work with more focus and clarity while directing our time and attention away from needless distractions.
- Simplifying our working and living environments lets us think more clearly by taking stock of the distractions that surround us.
- Clearing our minds using waiting-for, task, and worry lists lets us work with clarity and prevents unresolved mental loops from interrupting our focus throughout the day.
- Becoming good custodians of our attentional space—by making our work more complex when necessary and by expanding the limits of our attention—helps us properly manage our limited attention.

In the beginning of this book you may recall that I made a few lofty claims about how transformative it can be to purposefully manage your attention. If you've acted upon the advice so far, I think you'll find what I did: that your work and your life have been positively changed as a result of this practice.

As you've acted upon the advice in the first five chapters, I hope you've already become more productive, more engaged with your work and life, and a clearer and calmer thinker. You probably also remember more and view your work and life as more meaningful. All three measures of the quality of your attention have also likely increased—you spend more of your time deliberately; you are able to focus longer in one sitting; and your mind doesn't wander from your intentions nearly as much.

There is a wealth of research on how we can best focus, and in the first five chapters I've done my best to summarize it in a way that is both practical and tactical. I hope you'll agree: attention is the most important ingredient we have to living a good, productive life.

THE POWER OF MIND WANDERING

To this point in the book I've discussed only the negative effects of a wandering mind. At times when we need to focus, these mental strolls can undermine our productivity.

However, this mind-wandering mode—when we scatter our attention and focus—can also be immensely powerful. In fact, it's so powerful that I've devoted the second part of *Hyperfocus* to it. I call this mode "scatterfocus," because in it, our attention scatters to focus on nothing in particular. While hyperfocus involves directing your attention outward, scatterfocus is about directing it inward, inside your own mind.

Just as hyperfocus is the most *productive* mode of the brain, scatterfocus is the most *creative*. Scatterfocus can derail our productivity when our original intent is to focus, but when we're coming up with a creative solution to a problem, planning for our future, or making a difficult decision, it is just as essential as hyperfocus. We can harness the remarkable benefits of scatterfocus by practicing intentional mind wandering.

Learning how to use each mode intelligently will make you more productive, creative, and happy.

Let's dive into this second mental mode now. As you'll quickly see, hyperfocus and scatterfocus can work hand in hand in some truly remarkable ways.

PART II

SCATTERFOCUS

YOUR BRAIN'S HIDDEN CREATIVE MODE

Not all those who wander are lost.

—J. R. R. Tolkien

INTRODUCING SCATTERFOCUS

The second part of this book is devoted to the power of mind wandering and directing your attention inward.

Yes, you heard that right—after encouraging you in the first part of the book to rid yourself of that style of thinking, I'm about to explain the strengths of mind wandering. Part of its bad reputation is warranted: when our intention is to focus, daydreaming can destroy our productivity. But daydreaming is immensely potent when our intention is to solve problems, think more creatively, brainstorm new ideas, or recharge. As far as boosting our creativity is concerned, mind wandering is in a league of its own.

Think back to your last creative insight—chances are you weren't hyperfocusing on one thing. In fact, you probably weren't focused on much at all. You may have been taking an extra-long shower, having a walk during a lunch break, visiting a museum, reading a book, or relaxing on the beach with a drink or two. Maybe you were sipping your morning coffee. Then, like a flash of lightning, a brilliant idea struck out of nowhere. Your brain mysteriously chose this moment, when you were resting and recharging, to connect a few of the constellations of dots—let's consider a "dot" to be any idea or piece of information you remember—swirling in your head.

Just as hyperfocus is your brain's most productive mode, **scatterfocus** is its most creative.

Entering scatterfocus mode is easy: you simply let your mind be. Just as you hyperfocus by intentionally directing your attention toward one thing, you scatterfocus by deliberately letting your mind wander. You enter this mode whenever you leave attentional space free around what you're doing in the moment—whether going for a run, biking, or investing time in anything that doesn't consume your full attentional space.

When it comes to productivity and creativity, scatterfocus enables you to do three powerful things at once.

First, as I'll discuss in this chapter, it allows you to set intentions and plan for the future. It's impossible to set future intentions when you're immersed in the present. By stepping back and directing your attention inward, you're able to switch off autopilot and consider what to do next. Your brain automatically plans for the future when you rest—you just need to give it the space and time to do so.

Second, scatterfocus lets you recharge. Focusing on tasks all day consumes a good deal of mental energy, even when you're managing and defending your attentional space using the tactics set out in part 1. Scatterfocus replenishes that supply so you can focus for longer.

Third, scatterfocus fosters creativity. The mode helps you connect old ideas and create new ones; floats incubating thoughts to the surface of your attentional space; and lets you piece together solutions to problems. Scattering your attention and focusing on nothing in particular supercharges the dot-connecting powers of your brain. The more cre-

ativity your job or a project requires, the more you should deliberately
deploy scatterfocus.

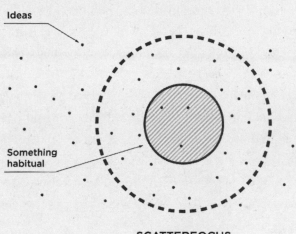

Ideas

Something
habitual

SCATTERFOCUS

WHY WE'RE AVERSE TO SCATTERFOCUS

Despite the productive and creative benefits of scatterfocus, most of us
are somewhat hesitant to engage this mode. While it's easy to get excited about becoming highly productive and hyperfocused, scattering
our attention is less exciting, at least on the surface. When we're surrounded by so many novel and stimulating objects of attention, most
of us don't want to be left alone with our thoughts.

In one recent survey, 83 percent of Americans responded that they
didn't spend *any* time whatsoever "relaxing or thinking" in the twenty-
four-hour period before they were surveyed. Another study sought to
measure exactly how resistant participants were to mind wandering. In
the first stage of the study, researchers attached two shock electrodes
to participants' ankles, zapped them, and then asked how much the
participants would pay to not receive the shock again. Around three

quarters of the group agreed they'd pay to not receive the shock again. In the second stage, participants were left alone with their thoughts for fifteen minutes. The researchers kept the electrodes on during that time, on the off chance anyone wanted to shock himself again, saving himself from his own thoughts. This is where the study gets interesting, and somewhat sad. A full *71 percent* of men in the study chose to self-administer an electric shock when left alone with their thoughts. Women fared better: only 26 percent chose to shock themselves again. (Take from these findings what you will.) This pattern held true regardless of age, education, economic status, and distraction level of the participants. The results are especially depressing when you consider that researchers allowed participants to proceed to this second stage only if they agreed to pay to not receive the shock again—anyone who didn't mind the shock was rejected.

If you read a lot of books like this one, you're probably familiar with the concept that our brains are wired for survival and reproduction— not to do knowledge work day in and day out. We focus on certain objects of attention by default, and doing so is what has allowed the human species to survive. We've already discussed the first type of object of attention that draws us in: anything that's *novel*. This is what makes our smartphones and other devices so enticing, while we find less novel tasks—like writing a report—boring, regardless of how much they lead us to accomplish.

We're also more likely to focus on anything that's *pleasurable* or *threatening*. This is where the survival instinct kicks in. Pleasures like sex and overeating have enabled us to reproduce and store fat for when food inevitably became scarce. Focusing on the threats in our environment, like the snake slithering nearby as our early ancestors built a fire, enabled us to live another day. We've crafted the world around us to cater to these cravings for novel, pleasurable, and threatening objects of attention. Consider this the next time you turn on the TV, open

YouTube, read a news website, or check social media—these outlets provide a steady fix of all three.

Today the balance of these three objects of attention has been tipped. We're continually surrounded by novel distractions, pleasures are plentiful, and legitimate threats are few and far between. The wiring in our brain that in our evolutionary past led us to store sugars and have sex as a survival mechanism now leads us to overindulge in fast food and pornography. Continually scanning for threats is what compels us to dwell on that one negative email or overthink a careless offhand comment from our boss. What once aided our chances at survival now sabotages our productivity and creativity in the modern world. It makes our most urgent tasks feel a lot more important than they actually are.

We're also prone to falling prey to what's novel, pleasurable, and threatening when we let our mind wander and turn our attention inward. Our greatest threats, worries, and fears no longer reside in our external environment but within the depths of our own consciousness. When our mind wanders, it slips into a pattern of ruminating on the stupid things we've said, the arguments we've won and lost, and worries about work and money. This is also true of pleasurable thoughts— we daydream of memorable meals, recall memories from a great vacation, or fantasize about how great we'd feel if we had come up with a witty retort to something said earlier. The next time you meditate (if you've begun to do so), pay attention to how your mind is naturally drawn to the threats, pleasures, and novel ideas floating in your head.

But in practice we don't actually experience negative mind-wandering episodes that often. Our mind primarily wanders to the negative when we're thinking about the past, but we wander to the past just *12 percent of the time*—the remainder is spent thinking about the present and the future, which makes scatterfocus remarkably productive. While our evolutionary history leads us to think about the novel and the negative, it has also wired our brain for profound creativity whenever we turn our attention inward. I'd argue that our ability to do so is practically a superpower.

Compared with other mammals, our ability to think about something that's not immediately in front of us is fairly unique.* It affords us the ability to plan for the future, learn from the past, and have daydreams that spawn remarkable insights. It helps us search inwardly for solutions to external situations—whether we're solving a math problem or telling the server how we usually take our eggs. Most remarkable, scatterfocus enables us to step back from life and to work and live more intentionally.

OH, THE PLACES OUR MIND GOES

In writing *Hyperfocus* I've had the opportunity to read hundreds, if not thousands, of studies related to attention management. Of all the research I encountered, my absolute favorite study looks at where our mind goes when it wanders. It was conducted by Benjamin Baird and Jonathan Schooler from the University of California at Santa Barbara and Jonathan Smallwood from the University of York. Their work is absolutely fascinating and provides scientific evidence for what makes scatterfocus so fruitful.

When your mind wanders, it visits three main places: the past, the present, and the future. This is precisely why scattering your attention

---

* There are exceptions to this rule: one study has observed that the western scrub jay tends to cache food for future meals because of its previous experience of having food stolen. This, according to the study's authors, "challenges the hypothesis that [the ability to future plan] is unique to humans." And another study found that "antelope and salamanders can predict the consequences of events they've experienced before." Whatever ability animals have to plan for and think about the future, however, seems rudimentary and limited.

allows your creativity to flourish as you travel through time and connect what you've learned to what you're doing or what you want to
achieve. This enables you to work with greater intention as you consider your future and think about what you should be doing in the
present to make it a reality.

Even though we spend just 12 percent of our scatterfocus time
thinking about the past, we're more likely to remember these thought
episodes, compared with when we think about the present or future.
(Fun fact: 38 percent of our past-related thoughts connect with
earlier-in-the-day events, 42 percent relate to the previous day's, and 20
percent involve ruminating on what happened in the more distant
past.) Our mind is wired to not only perceive but also remember
threats, like that one negative email that we can't forget. (It does this
so we learn from our mistakes, though it becomes annoying when it
throws random memories at us throughout the day.) On some level,
these past thoughts speak to the power of scatterfocus: when we daydream, we often experience our thoughts as if they were real. Cringeworthy memories strike from out of the blue, hijack our attention, and
lead us to tense up at the stupid stuff we've said and done.*

In addition to thinking about the past, our mind wanders to the
present 28 percent of the time. While we're not moving our work
forward during these wanderings, they can still be productive. Thinking abstractly about what's in front of us lets us consider alternate

---

* Our brain's default network—the network that we fire up as we enter into scatterfocus—
is extraordinarily powerful, and not just because it leads us to experience thoughts as
if they were real. Abnormal activity in the network—in particular an inability to
suppress the network—is associated with depression, anxiety, ADHD, posttraumatic
stress, autism, schizophrenia, Alzheimer's, and dementia. Generally, more activity in this
region of your brain is beneficial: one study found that "when people with higher IQ
scores [rest their attention,] the [default mode] connectivity in their brains, especially for
long-range connections, is stronger than that measured in the brains of people with average IQ."

approaches to the problems we're facing—like how we can best approach an awkward conversation to tell a coworker that he should be wearing deodorant. Wandering thoughts about what we're currently working on usually prove to be fairly productive—we need to reflect on our tasks in order to work more deliberately. Neurologically speaking, it's impossible to both focus on something and reflect on that thing at the same time. This makes entering scatterfocus critical. Without entering scatterfocus mode, you never think about the future. It's only once you step back from writing an email, drafting a paper, or planning your budget that you can consider alternative approaches to the task.

Finally, our mind wanders to think about the future *48 percent* of the time—more than our past and present thinking combined.* We usually think about the immediate future: 44 percent of our future thoughts concern a time later the same day, and 40 percent tomorrow. Most of this time is spent planning. Because of this, scatterfocus enables us to act more intelligently and more intentionally.

Every moment of our lives is like a Choose Your Own Adventure story—continually offering different options that allow us to define our future path. Scatterfocus lets us better imagine these paths: Should we talk to the good-looking person sitting alone across the coffee shop? Should we accept that job offer? How should we order our eggs? This mode also enables us to better weigh the consequences of each decision and path. In thinking about the future, we flick off autopilot mode and have the space to step back and consider how we want to act before our habits and routines make the decision for us.

Researchers refer to our mind's propensity to future-wander as our

---

* You may have noticed these percentages don't add up to 100 percent—the remaining 16 percent of the time our mind is somewhere else, like when it's connecting ideas or is dull or blank.

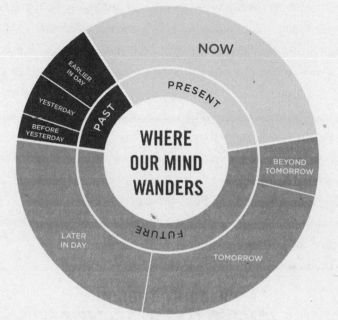

"prospective bias." This tendency is what leads us to spend half of our scatterfocus time planning.* We spend hardly any time thinking about the future when we're focused, while in scatterfocus mode we're *fourteen times* more likely to have these thoughts. Scatterfocus lets us work with greater intention because our mind automatically contrasts the future we desire against the present we need to change to make that future a reality. We consider our goals only about 4 percent of the time when we're immersed in what we're doing, while in scatterfocus mode we think about them 26 percent of the time. The more time you spend

* This prospective bias may be another reason we prefer distracting ourselves with Facebook over letting our mind wander. It's what makes us want to understand and predict the future. Seeing status updates from friends helps us understand the future much better—mind-wandering researchers say this is one of the reasons we fill our daydreaming time with stimulating distractions instead.

scatterfocusing between tasks—rather than indulging in distractions—the more thoughtful and productive your actions become.

As well as helping you plan for the future, recharge, and connect ideas, research suggests that scatterfocus mode also leads you to

- become more self-aware;
- incubate ideas more deeply;
- remember and process ideas and meaningful experiences more effectively;
- reflect on the meaning of your experiences;
- show greater empathy (scatterfocus gives you the space to step into other people's shoes); and
- become more compassionate.

THE THREE STYLES OF SCATTERFOCUS

In one respect scatterfocus is an odd mental mode to write about, as you need few instructions for how to let your mind wander. While hyperfocusing can be difficult, we already spend 47 percent of our day in something similar to scatterfocus mode without any effort, whenever our focus lapses and our attention wanders.

There are two ways your mind wanders: unintentionally and intentionally. Unintentional wandering takes place without your awareness, when you don't choose to enter into the mode. This is where I draw the line between mind wandering and scatterfocus. **Scatterfocus is always intentional.**

It may sound odd to release your grip on your attention *intentionally.* But in practice, there are other mental states in which you have even less control over your attention—including in hyperfocus.

Two of the most preeminent researchers in the field of mind wandering are Jonathan Smallwood and Jonathan Schooler, and they both agree on this point. When I chatted with him, Smallwood gave the example of watching a movie: "Let's say you sit down to watch *Pulp Fiction*. Quentin Tarantino has organized the entire movie to constrain your thoughts. You don't need to do anything as you watch the film— this is what makes the experience so relaxing. He controls your train of thought."

Research also suggests that we notice where our mind wanders around half of the time. We don't work with nearly this much awareness when focused on something. Schooler goes even further than Smallwood, arguing that one of the biggest misconceptions we have about mind wandering today is that "all mind wandering goes on without awareness, without intention."

Intention is what makes scatterfocus so powerful. This mode is always deployed deliberately—and involves making a concerted effort to notice where your mind goes.

I've found it helpful to distinguish among a few different styles of scatterfocus:

1. **Capture mode:** Letting your mind roam freely and capturing whatever comes up.
2. **Problem-crunching mode:** Holding a problem loosely in mind and letting your thoughts wander around it.
3. **Habitual mode:** Engaging in a simple task and capturing the valuable ideas and plans that rise to the surface while doing it. Research has found this mode is the most powerful.

Of the three styles, capture mode is best for identifying what's on your mind; problem-crunching mode is best for mulling over a specific problem or idea; and habitual mode is best for recharging and connecting the greatest number of ideas.

Capture Mode

As I mentioned in chapter 5, clearing your mind of open loops is a powerful productivity tactic. The fewer to-dos, calendar appointments, and unresolved commitments you keep stored in your mind, the fewer things there are to fill your attentional space as you try to focus.

For years I have been scheduling one or two fifteen-minute chunks of time each week to let my mind wander freely, during which I capture any valuable and actionable material. This practice is as simple as sitting with coffee, a pen, and a notebook and waiting to see what rises to the surface of my consciousness. By the end of the process, my notebook is invariably full: I've scribbled the names of people I should follow up with, stuff I've been waiting to do (and also follow up about), a list of people I should reconnect with, solutions to problems, tasks I've forgotten, house chores, intentions I should set, and more. I usually feel energized at the end of this little ritual because I've given my mind a break.

As discussed in chapter 4, unresolved tasks, projects, and commitments weigh heavily on our mind, perhaps because our brain views them as threats. In capture mode, any unresolved ideas or projects move to the forefront of your mind, ready to be written down and acted upon later. Our mind's propensity to wander toward these unresolved ideas is, in part, what makes scatterfocus so valuable—the open loops become much more accessible.

By way of example, I just put my computer to sleep, set a timer for fifteen minutes, and captured everything that rose to the surface of my mind. In that short period I noted the following to-do items:

- Map a time line of when I'll be done writing *Hyperfocus*.
- Contact my editor about adding a name to the acknowledgments section of my previous book.

- Remember to pick up my police check today (for a summer camp I volunteer for).
- Bring that police check to Ottawa this weekend.
- Complete the next module of the coding course I'm taking this evening.
- Book a massage for later this week.
- Make a list of the big things I need to wrap up today: finish this section of the book, do an hour of boredom experimentation, and write a quick newsletter for my website soliciting ideas for that experiment.

In addition to capturing these tasks, my mind mainly wandered to places you'd expect: mostly to the future and to the present, with some time pondering the past too. It's worth noting that I repeated this same capture ritual only a few days later and still managed to fill a few pages.

Of the three styles of scatterfocus, you'll probably find capture mode to be the most aversive—at least initially. Many people find the process boring, but this is precisely what leads your mind to wander and creates the space for ideas to rise to the surface of your attentional space. Cutting yourself off from distractions naturally turns your attention inward, as your thoughts become more interesting than anything in your external environment.

Problem-Crunching Mode

Problem-crunching mode is most useful when you're brainstorming a solution to a specific problem.

To enter this mode, hold a problem in your mind and let your thoughts wander around it, turn it over, and explore it from different angles. Whenever your mind ventures off to think about something unrelated or gets stuck on one point, gently nudge your attention back to what you intended to think about, or the problem you intended to solve.

Problem-crunching mode enables you to solve complicated problems more creatively—providing nonlinear solutions you wouldn't necessarily arrive at while logically brainstorming with a pen and a sheet of paper. Since you'll experience the same problem-solving benefits (and then some) when scatterfocusing on a habitual task, I recommend using the problem-crunching mode sparingly—save it for the largest problems you're processing. For example, it may be worth deploying when you're

- pondering whether to accept a new job and leave your current one;
- crafting a thoughtful email to your company's leadership team;
- considering a difficult relationship decision;
- brainstorming how you'll expand your business;
- deciding among three different homes to buy; or
- choosing between several potential hires for your team.

I went into problem-crunching mode constantly when coming up with the structure for this book; I would do so while canoeing, or I would walk around town with only a small notepad in my pocket. Once I had my structure, and before pitching the book to my publisher, I had around 25,000 words of research notes that weren't organized in the slightest. In my head the ideas were just as jumbled. I decided to put the research to the test and scatter my attention, hoping to give my mind the space it needed to connect the ideas I had captured. I printed my research notes—it's helpful to review problems before entering into problem-crunching mode—and then let my mind wander around them for an hour or two at a time on nature walks, while listening to music, or on airplanes. I slowly untangled my notes over the course of several weeks, shaping them into something that resembled a book.

Problem-crunching mode gives your mind the space and freedom to make these large leaps in your thinking. Try entering this mode if you haven't been able to solve a specific, nonlinear problem in a traditional way. I usually enter problem-crunching mode for thirty to sixty minutes at a time—I get restless if it's any longer. Test it and see what works for you.

Habitual Mode

Habitual scatterfocus is the most powerful style of this mode, and it's the one I recommend practicing the most often. (I'm covering it last in case you're tempted to gloss over the others, which are fruitful, but in different ways.)

As with the other modes, habitual scatterfocus is fairly easy: you simply do something habitual that doesn't consume your complete attention. This gives your mind space to wander and connect ideas. Doing this is beneficial for countless reasons.

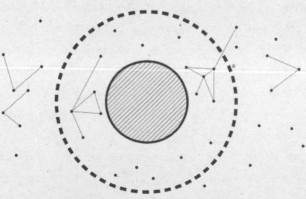

HABITUAL SCATTERFOCUS

For starters, **scatterfocus mode is actually fun** when you're engaged in a habitual activity you find pleasurable. Wandering your mind around one idea or capturing your thoughts can sometimes feel tedious, but when you do something habitual that you enjoy—like walking to get a coffee, woodworking, or swimming laps—scatterfocus becomes significantly more enjoyable. The happier you are in scatterfocus mode, the more benefits you'll reap. An elevated mood actually *expands the size of your attentional space*, which leads you to think more expansively. Your attentional space is just as essential in scatterfocus mode as it is in hyperfocus mode—it's the scratch pad your brain uses to connect ideas. A positive mood also allows your mind to wander more productively, as you're dwelling less on the negative past. You also think about the future more frequently when doing something pleasing—your brain's prospective bias grows even stronger. In addition, since doing a simple, pleasurable activity takes so little effort (and self-regulation), you can recharge at the same time you scatter your attention.

As well as being more fun, **habitual tasks have been shown to yield the greatest number of creative insights** when compared with switching to another demanding task, resting, or taking no break whatsoever. This holds especially true when you're stepping back from a problem—whether you're stumped on how to conclude a short story or considering the phrasing of an important report. It's also easier to stay aware of your thoughts when doing something habitual, as there's greater attentional space available to house your intention of being more aware of your thoughts. Again, this awareness is key: a creative thought is useless if it goes unnoticed.

Habitual tasks also encourage your mind to *continue* wandering. When you let your mind rest and wander, chances are you'll want to continue this scatterfocus exercise until you've finished whatever you started. A habitual task acts as a sort of "anchor" that guides your mind until you've completed the work. This enables you to keep going for longer.

To practice habitual scatterfocus, pick something simple that you enjoy doing. Then carry out that one task—and nothing else—until your mind wanders. The simpler the task, the better—going for a walk will unearth greater insights and connect more ideas than listening to music or reading a book. Good ideas will rise to the surface of your mind so long as you have attention to spare.

If you notice your mind has wandered to the past or to another unproductive place, allow it to wander (or, if you want, guide it to think of something else if it has gone to an unproductive place). This is where problem-crunching and habitual scatterfocus differ: in problem-crunching mode, you bring your thoughts back to the problem you're tackling; in habitual mode, you pretty much let your mind roam free.

You can also practice habitual scatterfocus with mandatory tasks that are already part of your day. There is a beautiful simplicity in doing one easy thing at a time, like drinking a cup of coffee, walking to work, or doing the laundry. Scatterfocus becomes most important in the moments between tasks. Stimulating devices and distractions don't only derail our focus—like water, they seep into the gaps in our schedule, stealing the valuable time and attention we would normally spend planning for the future and connecting ideas.

A primary reason many of us feel burned out is that we never give our attention a rest. Try this today: don't bring your phone with you the next time you walk to get a coffee or eat your lunch. Instead, let your mind wander. The effect of this simple decision alone is noticeable. If you don't check your phone each time a dinner date gets up from the table to go to the restroom, that meal will become more meaningful and memorable. By giving your attention a break, you'll have the attentional space to reflect on the conversation you've been having and what the other person means to you.

At the risk of repeating this too often, **the key to practicing habitual scatterfocus is to frequently check what thoughts and ideas are in your attentional space.** This is especially important with habitual scatterfocus, since more things are vying for your attention simultaneously. Keep this advice in mind when it's easy to become engrossed in the habitual task you've chosen. Sometimes I'll enter habitual scatterfocus by playing a simple, repetitive video game on my iPad. The game frees my mind to wander and think positively, and I come up with a remarkable number of ideas in the process. (Who said video games have to be unproductive?) Because I can play the game out of habit, I have some attention to spare—but I absolutely *have to* remember to continue to check what's occupying my attentional space, since the game is such a novel and pleasurable object of attention. Without this regular check-in, the experience is largely a waste of time and attention.

As with the other two styles of scatterfocus, make sure you have a notepad nearby when you enter habitual scatterfocus. You'll need it.

> **If you haven't already, schedule time to experiment with these scatterfocus modes.** This book is useful only if you try out its advice. Block a time in your calendar to enter capture or problem-crunching mode, or choose something simple you love doing every day, or something enjoyable you have to do, to let your mind wander in habitual scatterfocus mode. Then capture the valuable material that comes up and the ideas you connect. While your mind may already wander throughout the day, chances are most of that time is neither fun nor intentional. Set a goal to enter into the mode intentionally today, even if just for a few minutes. Jonathan Schooler supports this idea. As he told me, "I wish everyone knew how to experiment with the idea

themselves. Each one of us has such a unique relationship to mind wandering—and mind wandering can serve every one of us differently. We all need to figure out how it helps us in our own life, so we can take even more advantage of it. The beautiful thing is that it is a private experience that you can watch and introspect on yourself."

HOW HYPERFOCUS HELPS YOU SCATTERFOCUS

There are numerous ways to guide your mind to wander *even more* productively when practicing intentional scatterfocus. Luckily, you learned them all in the first part of the book!

In many ways, hyperfocus and scatterfocus couldn't be more different. Hyperfocus is about focusing on one thing; scatterfocus is about focusing on nothing in particular. With hyperfocus you direct your attention outward; with scatterfocus you direct your attention inward. One is about attention; the other is about inattention. On a neurological level, the two mental modes are even *anticorrelated*—when the brain network that supports scatterfocus is activated, activation in your hyperfocus network plummets, and vice versa.* All that said, the two modes of your brain reinforce each other—especially as you enter into each mode with intention. This makes it important to deliberately practice both modes.

---

* If you're curious, your brain's "task-positive" network supports hyperfocus, and your "task-negative," or "default mode," network supports scatterfocus. Your task-positive network is activated when you're paying attention to something external, while your default mode network is activated when your internal focus is high.

Practicing hyperfocus—and deliberately managing your attention—provides a host of benefits: expanding your attentional space so you can focus on more tasks simultaneously, improving your memory, and letting you become more aware of the thoughts flying around your head. As it turns out, all three of these are beneficial in scatterfocus mode.

The size of your attentional space is one of the biggest determinants of how fruitful your scatterfocus episodes will be. The bigger the better, as it will allow you to keep more in mind while scatterfocusing. Attentional space is integral to both mental modes: in hyperfocus, what you're working on fills it; in scatterfocus mode, it lets you construct new ideas and think cohesively about the future.

Deliberately managing your attention also leads you to remember more. This is the second way in which regularly practicing hyperfocus helps: the more information you gather and remember when focused, the better you are at constructing ideas and future events in scatterfocus mode. As a recent review in the scientific journal *Nature* put it, it's "helpful to think of the brain as a fundamentally prospective organ that is designed to use information from the past and the present to generate predictions about the future. Memory can be thought of as a tool used by the prospective brain to generate simulations of possible future events."

Remembering the past helps us imagine the future, as it's impossible to piece together ideas and information we haven't paid attention to in the first place. The better we manage our attention when we're focused, the more information we'll have to draw upon when we're not. A later chapter is devoted to how important it is to choose what you consume and pay attention to: just as you are what you eat, when it comes to the information you consume, you are what you choose to focus on. Consuming valuable material in general makes scatterfocus sessions even more productive.

A third idea we've already covered is the importance of meta-awareness and continually checking what's consuming your attentional space. This not only enables you to focus more deeply but also helps you to scatterfocus.

As you might have experienced, it can take a few minutes to notice your mind has wandered, even during meditation. A study conducted by Jonathan Schooler found that we notice our mind has wandered, on average, just 5.4 times every hour. Remember the earlier figure that indicated that our mind wanders 47 percent of the time. Taken together, these figures show just how long our mind can wander without our awareness. There's an interesting reason that it takes us awhile to realize that our mind has wandered. As one study put it, its doing so "can hijack the very brain regions that are necessary for recognizing its occurrence." This makes a regular check of what's occupying our attention doubly important.

The more often you do this check, the more productive your mind-wandering episodes will be. You will be better able to move your thoughts away from the past and instead think about current ideas and the future. As with expanding the size of your attentional space, practicing meta-awareness has been shown to make scatterfocus mode significantly more positive and constructive.

RETHINKING BOREDOM

Answer this question honestly: When was the last time you were bored?

Really think about it. Can you remember?

Chances are it was a long time ago, maybe before welcoming devices into your life. Never in human history have we divided our attention among so many things. In the moment this can feel like a benefit—we always have something to do—but the disadvantage is that distracting devices have basically eliminated boredom from our lives.

You might be asking: Isn't ridding ourselves of boredom a positive

change? Not necessarily. Boredom is the feeling we experience as we
transition into a lower level of stimulation. It most often appears when
we are *suddenly* forced to adapt to this lower level—when we find ourselves looking for something to do on a Sunday afternoon or switch
from writing an email to sitting in a grueling meeting:

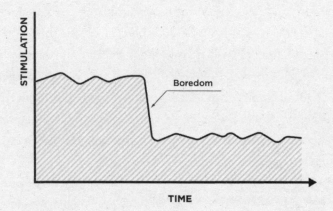

It's no wonder that boredom eludes us when we always have a device
to reach for or a distracting website to visit—there is always something
to amuse us in the moment. As a consequence, we don't often find
ourselves having to adjust to a lower level of stimulation. In fact, we
frequently have to yank our focus away from these devices when it's
time to actually get something done.

I'm a big fan of experimenting with my own advice, because many
tips that sound good on the surface don't actually work in practice. I
recently did so to determine, once and for all, whether boredom is, in
fact, a positive thing. Is boredom productive in small doses? How does
it differ from scatterfocus? Are we right to resist it?

During a monthlong experiment I intentionally made myself bored
for an hour a day. In that period I shut off all distractions and spent

my time and attention on an excruciatingly boring task, based on the thirty weirdest ideas suggested by my website readers:

1. Reading the iTunes terms and conditions
2. Staring at the ceiling
3. Watching C-SPAN 3
4. Waiting on hold with Air Canada's baggage claim department
5. Watching C-SPAN 2
6. Watching my turtle, Edward, swim back and forth in her tank
7. Staring at a slowly rotating fan blade
8. Painting a tiny canvas with one color
9. Watching paint dry
10. Looking out my office window
11. Removing and counting the seeds on a strawberry with a pair of tweezers
12. Watching grass grow
13. Staring out a train window
14. Watching an online chess tournament
15. Watching one cloud in the sky
16. Waiting at the hospital
17. Watching a dripping faucet
18. Ironing every piece of clothing I own
19. Counting the 0s in the first 10,000 digits of pi
20. Watching my girlfriend read
21. Making dots on a sheet of paper
22. Eating alone in a restaurant, without a book or phone
23. Reading Wikipedia articles about rope
24. Watching a clock
25. Watching every file transfer from my computer to an external hard drive (and back)

26. Peeling exactly five potatoes
27. Watching a pot boil
28. Attending a church service in Latin
29. Watching C-SPAN
30. Moving small rocks from one place to another, repeatedly

A few times each hour I randomly sampled what was going on in my head: whether my thoughts were positive, negative, or neutral; whether my mind was focused on something or was wandering; how constructive the thoughts were; how I felt; and how much time I estimated had passed since the previous sample.

Some of the findings from this experiment were unsurprising. As soon as my external environment became less stimulating, I naturally turned my attention inward, where my thoughts were infinitely more interesting and stimulating. In this sense, boredom is really just unwanted scatterfocus. I still found my mind planning for the future, processing ideas, and bouncing between the past, present, and future, just as it does in habitual scatterfocus mode, but I didn't enjoy the process as much or have the desire to keep going.

The experiment also yielded a few unexpected side effects. One that made me feel especially uneasy was how, in the absence of stimulation, I instinctively looked for distractions to occupy my attention. Forced to remove the seeds of a strawberry with a pair of tweezers or read Wikipedia articles related to rope, I found myself looking for something, *anything* to do: a mess to clean, a device to pick up—any pacifier that would distract me from the thoughts in my head. If I had been able to administer myself an electric shock in that moment, I might have done it. Our mind is accustomed to constant stimulation and tends to seek it as if it were a universally good thing. It isn't.

It's not a coincidence that so many tactics in this book involve making your work and life less stimulating—the less stimulated you are, the more deeply you can think. Each time we eschew boredom for stimulation, we fail to plan, unearth ideas our mind has incubated, or recharge so we can work later with greater energy and purpose.

This is not to say boredom is totally useful. Unlike habitual scatterfocus, boredom makes us anxious, uneasy, and uncomfortable—feelings I constantly had during the experiment. More boredom is not something that I'd wish on anyone—but more mind wandering *is*. Fortunately our mind wanders to the same places during episodes of either scatterfocus or boredom, so scatterfocus is just as positive—it lets our mind wander while we become less stimulated, but it does so with purpose.

There used to be an app called Disk Defragmenter that came preinstalled on all Windows computers, back when every PC shipped with a slow, spinning hard disk. If your computer was running sluggishly, the program would dutifully rearrange the discontiguous blocks of files so they would be physically closer on the drive. This significantly sped up the computer, because the drive would no longer have to spin like crazy to search for the elements of a given file scattered across its platter.

Regardless of how technical you were, using the app was always oddly satisfying, and even visually pleasing, as it displayed an image of blocks strewn across a rectangle, which would be dutifully rearranged and cleaned up during the running of the program.

Our mind works in a similar way. We defragment our thoughts when we carve out space between tasks. This helps us think clearly and gives us extra attention to process relationships, experiences, ideas, and problems we can't figure out. In these moments, boredom and scatter-focus are powerful because they enable useful self-examination.

As I hope you'll agree, these activity gaps are just as valuable as the activities themselves. It's time to reclaim them.

RECHARGING YOUR ATTENTION

*Rest is not idleness, and to lie sometimes on the
grass under the trees on a summer's day, listening to
the murmur of water, or watching the clouds float
across the blue sky, is by no means a waste of time.*
—John Lubbock, in *The Use of Life*

WHEN YOU SHOULD RECHARGE

As well as enabling you to set intentions more often and improving your creativity, scatterfocus helps you recharge.

Our energy levels influence how well we're able to focus. You probably felt the effects of this the last time you missed a few hours of sleep or skipped your work breaks. Odds are that all three measures of the quality of your attention decreased: you couldn't focus for as long, you were distracted and sidetracked by other tasks or interests more frequently, and you found yourself working on autopilot more often.

The lesson of this chapter is simple: the more often we scatterfocus to replenish our mental energy, the more energy we have for our most important tasks. As our mental energy steadily depletes throughout the day, so too does our ability to focus. Recharging is critical and worth the time investment.

Research shows that attentional space expands and contracts in proportion to how much mental energy we have. Getting enough sleep, for example, can increase the size of attentional space by as much as *58 percent*, and taking frequent breaks can have the same effect. This impacts productivity: when attentional space is approximately 60 percent larger, productivity can grow by just as much, especially when we're working on a demanding task. The better rested we are, the more productive we become.

Hyperfocus can be pretty tiring—it requires that we regulate our behavior, which steadily drains a pool of limited energy. Eventually our energy wanes, and focusing on the task at hand becomes more difficult. Our attentional space contracts, and we need to recharge.

OUR ATTENTIONAL SPACE OVER TIME

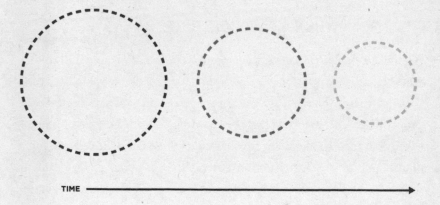

TIME

There are many signs that indicate you're running low on energy and should recharge your attention by deliberately entering scatter-focus mode:

- Switching often among tasks and being unable to sustain focus on one thing

- Losing your grip on your intentions and working in a more reactive way
- Getting tasks done at a noticeably slower rate (e.g., reading the same important email several times to comprehend it)
- Opting to do less important, more mindless work—like checking email, social media, etc.
- Unintentionally slipping into scatterfocus mode

TAKING MORE REFRESHING BREAKS

Many people burn through an inordinate amount of time doing work that doesn't make them happy. Doing work you love is significantly less exhausting than doing work you don't care about—focus always feels more forced for the latter. The more you care, the more mileage you'll get out of your attention. Research also suggests that your mind wanders less when you're doing something you genuinely enjoy.

In addition to scatterfocus's other benefits, practicing it provides a pocket of time in which you don't have to regulate your behavior, which is energy restorative. Practicing scatterfocus, even if just for five to ten minutes, lets your brain rest, which helps replenish your limited pool of mental energy.

Research has shown that a refreshing work break should have three characteristics. It should be

- low-effort and habitual;
- something you actually *want* to do; and
- something that isn't a chore (unless you genuinely enjoy doing the chore).

In short, your breaks should involve something that's pleasurably effortless.

Fun, leisurely work breaks provide the same remarkable benefits of the habitual scatterfocus mode: your mind will wander to the future as you create the attentional space for more ideas and insights. Fun breaks also energize you for when you do resume working.

Work breaks aren't generally as refreshing as they should be, as we immediately become too busy checking social media and the news and distracting ourselves in other ways without stepping back to actually let our minds rest. These "breaks" are effectively a code name for activities unrelated to our work—and because they still require our attention, we never truly have a chance to recharge. Instead of thinking clearly and deliberately when we resume working, we can muster the energy only to work on autopilot mode, checking if new emails came in and doing unnecessary and distracting work.

There are countless refreshing and enjoyable break activities, each of which will let you experience the immense benefits of habitual scatterfocus while not taking away from your ability to hyperfocus once the break ends.

Pick an activity you love, something you can do once or twice a day where you work. Set an intention to do the activity tomorrow. This could involve walking around the office, taking advantage of a gym nearby, or spending time with coworkers who energize you. These activities are a great way to give your mind a genuine break. Resist the urge to mindlessly distract yourself during this pocket of time. During my own work breaks I step back every hour or so to let my mind recharge. I love walking to and from the local coffee shop without my phone, working out at the gym, catching up with a colleague or two, or listening to a podcast.

Here are a few other break activities that have worked for me, and for the people I've coached:

- Going on a nature walk*
- Running outside or visiting the gym at work (if your company has one) or off-site
- Meditating (especially if your office has a relaxation room)
- Reading something fun and not work-related
- Listening to music, a podcast, or an audiobook
- Spending time with coworkers or friends
- Investing time in a creative hobby like painting, woodworking, or photography

When you choose a break activity you love, you can still experience the benefits of habitual scatterfocus while you rest and recharge.

TIMING

So when and how often should you step back from your work?

Because no two people are the same, the frequency and length of breaks depend on countless factors. Just as you had to try various alternatives to create a personalized distraction-free mode, experiment to learn what provides *you* with the most energy. For example, you may need to take breaks more often if you're an introvert whose work involves a great deal of social interaction with large groups of people. If you're an introvert who works in an open office, you may need to step back more frequently throughout the day as well.

---

* This book would be more than a thousand pages long if I covered every topic that contributed to promoting focus, but it's worth highlighting spending time in nature to help you feel rested and recharged. This activity makes you up to 50 percent better at creative problem-solving tasks, lowers levels of stress hormones in your body by around 16 percent, makes you calmer, and elevates your mood. One study even discovered that "[t]hose living on blocks with more trees showed a boost in heart and metabolic health equivalent to what one would experience from a $20,000 gain in income." We evolved to thrive in nature—not concrete jungles.

Frequent recharging may also be necessary if you find you aren't motivated by a particular project, or by your work in general. The more you need to regulate your behavior—to resist distractions and temptations or push yourself to get things done—the more often you'll need to recharge. (This is why deadlines can be so useful: they force you to focus on something.) Focus becomes effortless when you're working on a task that's intrinsically motivating— all the productivity advice in the world won't help if you can't stand your job.*

If you're in a management role, hiring people who deeply care about your company values is the best decision you can make. Managers often try to make their team more productive after the fact. They successfully hire highly skilled people, but ones who are doing the job only for a paycheck.

Research on the value of breaks points to two simple rules:

1. Take a break *at least* every ninety minutes.
2. Break for roughly fifteen minutes for each hour of work you do.

This may seem like a lot of time across an eight-hour workday, but it's approximately equivalent to taking a one-hour lunch break and a fifteen-minute break in the morning and afternoon. In most situations these two rules are practical and can be carried out without affecting your work schedule.

Why is ninety minutes the magic number? Our mental energy tends to oscillate in ninety-minute waves. We sleep in ninety-minute

---

* An interesting observation: the less a person is motivated by money, the more money they end up making in the end. Money, fame, and power are extrinsic goals—they're external to you and far less motivating than intrinsic goals, such as growth, community, and helping others.

cycles, moving between periods of light, deep, and REM sleep. Our energy continues to follow the same rhythm after we wake: we feel rested for around ninety minutes and then tired for a short period of time—around twenty to thirty minutes. A short break every ninety minutes or so takes advantage of these natural peaks and valleys in energy cycles. Take a break when you notice your focus dipping or after finishing a big task—doing so will mean you'll experience less attentional residue as you allow your mind to wander.

By taking strategic breaks we're able to use periods of greater mental energy for maximum productivity—and replenish our energy when it would naturally dip. Research shows we're more creative during these low-energy periods, as during them our brain is the least inhibited, which allows more ideas to rise to the surface. This makes low-energy moments perfect for scatterfocus. Start to pay attention to the ebb and flow of your energy levels in the morning, and make a concerted effort to step back when you feel your energy beginning to dip. Energy levels stabilize a bit more in the afternoon and dip less predictably—but it's worth sticking with a similar rhythm.

And why should we have a fifteen-minute break for each hour of work? There isn't a lot of reliable research on this subject, but one company did try to crunch the numbers. A time-tracking app called DeskTime—which automatically tracks the computer programs you have open so you can see at day's end how productive you were—assessed the break data for the most productive 10 percent of its users. They discovered that, on average, these users took a seventeen-minute break after every fifty-two minutes of work.

It's worth adapting your break schedule around your work habits. If you have a second tea or coffee in the morning, take it after ninety minutes of work and give your mind a legitimate rest during that time. Instead of eating a rushed lunch in front of your computer, take a *real* lunch break—one that will legitimately recharge you for the afternoon.

Leave your phone at the office and enter scatterfocus mode on a lunch-time run or while reading a good book, being sure to capture any thoughts and ideas you've been incubating. In the afternoon, grab a decaf coffee, or take advantage of your company's nap room, meditation space, or gym.

The best time to take a break is before you need to. Much as you're probably already dehydrated when you feel thirsty, your focus and productivity have likely already begun to falter by the time you feel fatigued.

SLEEP

Speaking of rest, it would be remiss of me to not discuss sleep.

I personally have a (granted, somewhat pseudoscientific) rule that I think is worth following when it comes to sleep: **For every hour of sleep you miss, you lose two hours of productivity the next day.** There's no scientific backing for this rule—as with breaks, we're all wired differently—but the amount of sleep we get matters a great deal, especially with regard to knowledge work. We lose more than we gain when we compromise our sleep to work longer hours.

The size of our attentional space can shrink by as much as 60 percent as the result of a sleep deficit—complex tasks can take more than twice as long when we're tired. We also become less self-aware and survey our attentional space less often. Working with a diminished attentional space is fine for mindless tasks like copying data into a spreadsheet, but our productivity is undercut when we try to focus on something complex. In most cases, we're better off working fewer hours and getting enough sleep than trying to do a full day's work while tired. Some people claim they're able to get by with less sleep than everyone else, but chances are either their work isn't as complex or they'd be capable of accomplishing even more if they were better rested. Even worse, a sleep deficit makes us perceive our productivity as being higher than it actually is.

Even though we spend about a third of our life in a basically comatose state, we understand very little of what happens during sleep. This is true for a number of reasons: our brains are inordinately complex, brain-scanning equipment is expensive, and the noise of the scanners tends to disrupt participants' later (and lighter) stages of sleep. The studies that do provide a glimpse into what happens in our brains as we sleep, however, are fascinating—especially the ones that examine the similarities between sleep and scatterfocus.

If you were to place someone who is dreaming and another person who is daydreaming into a brain-scanning machine, you'd notice something peculiar: the two brain scans would be eerily similar. Sleep dreaming and daydreaming in scatterfocus mode activate the same brain regions, though they're even more active while we're asleep. On a neurological level, dreaming is scatterfocus mode on steroids.

This makes sense when we consider the two modes. We feel recharged after episodes of both sleep and scatterfocus. Our minds wander to many of the same places whether we're sleeping or daydreaming—including past regrets, fantasies and anxieties about the future, and our relationships with other people (though our mind jumps among things a lot more when we're dreaming). The mind has a chance to defragment its thoughts during both sleep and mind-wandering episodes, as well as to consolidate the information it's been learning and processing. The brain also fires somewhat randomly in each mode, which can lead to breakthrough ideas (as well as to some random, useless material). It's no wonder countless great ideas have come to people in their sleep—including Paul McCartney's melody for "Yesterday," Dmitry Mendeleyev's idea for the periodic table of elements, and Jack Nicklaus's new and improved golf swing.

In addition to the productivity toll, the costs of working with a sleep deficit are numerous. Research shows that as we get less sleep, we also

- feel more pressure at work;
- focus for a shorter duration of time (*even less* than forty seconds);
- fire up social media sites more often;
- experience more negative moods;
- actively seek less demanding tasks (eliminating those that no longer fit into our shrunken attentional space); and
- spend more time online throughout the day.

This holds especially true for those aged nineteen to twenty-nine, a demographic that chooses to go to bed later than any other age cohort—around midnight, on average. Given that most of us need around eight hours of sleep, turning in at midnight doesn't exactly prepare us to be productive the following day, unless we have the flexibility to wake up late.

One of the best ways to get more sleep, and to increase the quality of your sleep, is to develop a solid nighttime ritual. Because our energy levels are depleted by the end of the day, we tend to spend a large amount of time then on autopilot mode. Establish a set routine that enables you to unwind before bed. Consider adding habits like reading, meditation, disconnecting, drinking a cup of herbal tea, or simply removing the TV from your bedroom. It's a convenient object of attention infinitely more stimulating than sleep. Getting to bed at a decent hour is the best way to get enough sleep. While most of us need to wake up by a certain time, our nightly routine is usually more flexible.

REST IS NOT IDLENESS

It often doesn't feel right to step back and rest when you have more work to do than time to do it—you may even feel twinges of guilt. This is usually just self-doubt rearing its ugly head: as you consider the opportunity costs of taking a break, you begin thinking of all the other things you *should* be working on instead. Taking a break *feels* less productive than getting real work done, so you feel at fault when you even *consider* stepping back.

This logic doesn't hold water in practice. In fact, taking a break is one of the most productive things you can do. As we've discussed, your brain has a limited pool of energy, and once that reserve is depleted, so too are your focus and productivity. Breaks not only allow you to recharge—they prevent you from hitting a wall.

Whenever we rest, we exchange our time for energy. This is true regardless of whether we're resting by taking a break or by getting a good night's sleep. This time investment doesn't evaporate into the ether, and in reality, you should feel guilty about *not* taking breaks.

I've asked you to look back at your work and life quite often in this book, such as suggesting that you think of when you felt the most focused and creative. There's a reason for this: you can learn a lot through a little introspection. If you want to become more productive, creative, or engaged with your work, the truth is you already have a huge amount of data at your disposal. All you have to do is reflect on when you were the most productive, creative, or happy and consider the conditions that led to that state.

It's worth doing a similar exercise here. Think back to when you last approached your work with the greatest energy. Maybe there was a stretch of time when you had a habit of exercising at lunch or took more breaks than usual. How much were you able to accomplish on those days?

Taking more breaks will absolutely lead you to work smarter and accomplish more—ironically, the busier you are, the more you need them. During times like this, the likeliness of being overwhelmed is higher, and you will benefit from the perspective scatterfocus provides.

This chapter is one of the shortest in the book, because the main idea is simple: scatterfocus mode helps us to recharge our ability to hyperfocus, in addition to letting us plan for the future and become more creative.

CONNECTING DOTS

It's not that I'm so smart; it's just that
I stay with problems longer.
—*Albert Einstein*

BECOMING MORE CREATIVE

As well as enabling you to plan for the future and replenish your supply
of mental energy, scatterfocus allows you to become more creative. You
can use scatterfocus mode to become more creative in two ways: first,
by connecting more dots; and second, by collecting more valuable
dots—a topic that will be covered in the next chapter.

Hyperfocus is about focusing on a single thing. This lets your brain
become productive, encode information and experiences so that you
remember them later, and engage with the world around you. In
scatterfocus mode you do the opposite: you zoom out and connect the
constellations of "dots" in your head (a "dot" being any piece of information you hold in your mind).

On a neurological level, our brain is a constellation of dot-filled
networks—and we're constantly adding more with every new experience. We gather dots when we're creating memories with loved ones,
studying history, or reading the biographies of people who lived
through it—which helps us understand the sequences of ideas that created the world we live in today. We accumulate dots with each mistake

we make (and learn from) and each time we're open enough to admit
that we're wrong—which replaces the obsolete dots in our mind with
new ones. We harvest dots with each enlightening conversation, which
permits us to gaze at the constellations of dots that live in the minds of
knowledgeable people or ones who see the world differently. Each dot
is encoded into our memory and available for later use.

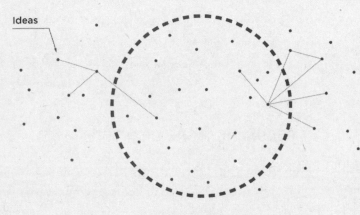

SCATTERFOCUS

The word that best describes how your brain looks when you enter
scatterfocus mode is "random." Scatterfocus lights up your brain's default network—the network it returns to when you're not focused on
something.* This network is widely distributed across the brain, as is
the information we've encoded into memory. One of the many reasons
scatterfocus leads to so many creative insights is that while in it, we
naturally begin to connect the scattered dots we've collected. As we

---

* In a strange bit of irony, the default network, which supports scatterfocus, was discovered serendipitously as well. At first the network was ignored. Then it was dismissed as
an experimental error—mere background noise in the brain-scanning machines. Eventually scientists discovered the error of their ways, and it has since emerged as a major
topic of study in the field of neuroscience.

cast a metaphorical net across our minds, fishing for novel connections, we connect ideas while we rest and plan for the future.

We're not always aware of the ideas our attentional space pans over as we move among our thoughts—like an iceberg that resides mostly underwater, much of this process takes place in the depths of our consciousness. Since we can focus on just a small amount of information at one time, only a few of the active connections in our minds can break into our attentional space. However, these random connections *do* get our attention when they become sufficiently activated. It's at this moment that we realize we should hire Cheryl instead of Jim, map the intentions we should set for later, or arrive at a sudden eureka insight.

INSIGHT TRIGGERS

Uncompleted tasks and projects weigh more heavily on our minds than ones we've finished—focus comes when we close these distracting open loops. We're wired to remember what we're in the middle of more than what we've completed. In psychology circles this phenomenon is called the Zeigarnik effect, after Bluma Zeigarnik, the first person to study this concept. The Zeigarnik effect can be annoying when we're trying to focus, but the opposite is true when we scatter our attention. In fact, it leads to amazing insights into the problems we're incubating.

Chances are you've experienced a few eureka moments yourself. Maybe they struck while you were making breakfast, getting the mail, or walking through an art gallery. Your brain suddenly and unexpectedly found the solution to a problem you hadn't thought about for a few hours. In an instant, the puzzle pieces satisfyingly slid together and locked into place.

Two things were likely true at that moment: first, at that moment your insight was a response to a problem you were stuck on. Second, your mind was likely wandering while you were doing something that didn't require your full attention.

Thanks to the Zeigarnik effect, we store any and all problems currently stumping us at the front of our minds. Any open problem—an unfinished report, a decision we're in the middle of, or an important email we're responding to—is an open loop that our brain is desperate to close. As a consequence, we connect each new experience to these unresolved problems in order to unearth novel solutions. Habitual scatterfocus brings these connections into our attentional space.

When we're in habitual scatterfocus mode, potential insight triggers come from two places: our wandering minds themselves and the external environment. It's best to illustrate this with an example.

Let's say I invite you to my secret productivity-experiment lair. I offer you a seat, set a timer for thirty minutes, and ask you to solve this seemingly simple problem: The number 8,549,176,320 is probably the single most unique ten-digit number in the world. What makes it unlike any other number? Let's imagine you can't solve the problem in the allotted time—not unreasonable, given that this is a particularly tricky one. You leave frustrated, and the question continues to weigh on your mind: *What is so unusual about 8,549,176,320?*

By now you've reached an impasse and have encoded the problem into memory. You've started to see those digits whenever you close your eyes. (Naturally, the better you remember a complex problem, the greater your odds of coming up with a creative solution.) This particular brain teaser would probably never actually cause a high level of torment. But for the sake of this example, let's say it does.

Thanks to the Zeigarnik effect, your mind will automatically connect your new experiences to this problem, whether you realize it or not. You return to work, still frustrated, with the number imprinted on your brain. You find your mind returning to it periodically, sometimes even against your will. In fact, odds are that your mind will wander *more* often than usual—our thoughts drift more often when we're in the middle of solving a complex problem—which will cause you to make a higher-than-normal number of mistakes in your work.

Later in the day, you work on an activity that takes you into habitual scatterfocus mode: organizing your bookshelf in alphabetical order. You're putting away the book *The 80/20 Principle* by Richard Koch. As you do so, your mind processes where the book will be shelved.

Okay, ignore the word "the."

First value is 8, so I'll put it with the other books that start with a number.

Huh, the number in Chris's experiment was also an 8.

Like a lightning bolt, the solution hits you. You feel dozens of puzzle pieces sliding and locking into place in your mind.

8,549,176,320.

Eight, five, four, nine . . .

A, B, C, D, Eight, FIve, FOur, G, H . . .

The number in the experiment has every digit, arranged in alphabetical order!

As far as insight triggers go, this is a fairly straightforward one—usually they are more subtle, nudging your mind to think in a different direction and restructuring the mental dots that represent a problem. I designed this example to illustrate a simple concept: habitual scatterfocus lets our minds connect the problems we're tackling with what we experience, as well as where our minds happen to wander.

Insight is a notoriously difficult subject to study. To do so, you have to lead people to an impasse on a problem and maintain sufficient interest in it to make them want to solve it later. Luckily, you don't need the results of research to support these findings—you probably have enough data at your disposal in the form of your own past experiences.

I can't stress enough how remarkable insight triggers are. You may see a bird picking at a chip packet, which leads you to realize you should clear the chips you've been snacking on out of the kitchen so you can lose those final ten pounds. Intentionally daydreaming during your morning shower, you recall how you resolved a past work dispute and realize you can use the same technique today. Walking through a bookstore, you notice a cookbook, which reminds you that you were planning on replacing your kitchenware set—and that there's a store around the corner that sells them. The richer our environment, and the richer our experiences, the more insights we're able to unearth.

Look back at some of the greatest eureka moments in history. In addition to reaching an impasse with their problems, the famous thinkers arrived at solutions to them after being spurred by an external cue. Archimedes figured out how to calculate the volume of an irregular object when he noticed his bathwater overflowing. Newton came up with his theory of gravity when he saw an apple fall from a tree— probably the best-known insight trigger in history. For his habitual scatterfocus routine, renowned physicist and Nobel laureate Richard Feynman would sip 7UP at a topless bar, where he could "'watch the entertainment,' and, if inspiration struck, scribble equations on cocktail napkins."

CONNECTING EVEN MORE DOTS

Simply entering habitual scatterfocus mode will enable you to experience the remarkable benefits I've covered so far. But if you want to level up even further, here are six ways to do so.

1. Scatter your attention in a richer environment.

Being mindful of and controlling your environment is one of the most productive steps you can take. In addition to creating a focus-conducive environment (using the steps discussed in the first part of this book), you can also help surface scatterfocus insights by deliberately exposing yourself to new cues.

Immersing yourself in a setting that contains potential insight triggers is a powerful practice. A rich environment is one where you're constantly encountering new people, ideas, and sights. Break activities like walking through a bookstore or people-watching at a diner are far more valuable than those that don't carry any new potential cues. Adopt a mix of such activities—some that give your mind the space to wander and connect dots and others that expose your mind to new ideas you can connect later.

> **You can also use cues to *capture* everything you need to get done.** Walk around your house with a notepad and draw up a list of tasks that need to be completed. This list represents your external cues. You'll be able to capture just as much—if not more—valuable information if you do the same at the office or while browsing each folder on your computer. While this might feel overwhelming at first, you'll be able to better organize and prioritize everything on your plate. If you want to deepen your relationships with friends, scroll through the contacts app on your phone and take note of whom you haven't connected with in a while. If you want to develop deeper professional relationships, scroll through your LinkedIn contact list. Deliberately exposing yourself to new cues can help in these ways and more.

2. Write out the problems you're trying to crack.

I hit a major impasse when I pored through the 25,000 words of research notes I had collected for *Hyperfocus*: How could I reorganize these digital scribbles into something resembling a book? My outline document was essentially a 25,000-word problem statement. I printed and reviewed it regularly—noting at the top of the pages my biggest challenges, such as how I'd make the book practical, structure the manuscript, and present the research so that it was interesting.

Regularly reviewing these problems and the document itself kept the project fresh in my mind. Frequently entering habitual scatterfocus mode (including one afternoon during which I scanned the tables of contents of about a hundred books to see how they were structured) surrounded me with potential solution cues—I was scattering my attention in a richer environment. Eventually the answers came.

Writing down the detailed problems you're tackling at work and at home helps your mind continue to process them in the background. When you capture the tasks, projects, and other commitments on your plate, you're able to stop thinking about them and focus on your other work. The opposite is true when it comes to the problems you're in the middle of solving: recording them on paper helps you to better clarify, process, and remember them.

This same technique works for large projects—making an outline for how you'll write your thesis, remodel your kitchen, or staff your new team helps you process these ideas in the background so you can continue to collect and connect new dots related to the project.

Another powerful idea for the smaller nuts you're trying to crack: in addition to setting three next-day intentions at the end of the workday, note the largest problems you're in the middle of processing. You'll be surprised how many you figure out by the next morning.

3. Sleep on a problem.

As I mentioned earlier, dreaming is scatterfocus on steroids: while you're sleeping, your mind continues to connect dots.

There are countless examples of eureka insights that have struck people as they dreamed. To harness the power of sleep, Thomas Edison would go to bed holding a handful of marbles, and Salvador Dalí would doze off with a set of keys in his hand, dangling over a metal plate. Both men would continue holding the items during the lighter stages of sleep but drop them once they hit a deeper stage, which woke them up. This allowed them to capture whatever insight was on their mind in that moment. Edison put it memorably when he purportedly urged that you should "never go to sleep without a request to your subconscious."

Deep and freeform connections come especially strongly as you dream during the REM stage of sleep. One study that had participants incubate a problem found that during REM sleep, participants "showed enhanced integration of unassociated information," which helped them find a solution.

Sleep also helps you remember more—it consolidates the dots you've accumulated over the course of the day into long-term memory and intentionally forgets the less important and irrelevant dots you encountered. You absorb a lot of "noise" over the course of the day, and sleep gives your brain the chance to dispose of dots that don't have a valuable connection to the others in your mind.

To invest in a good night's sleep and to use this tool to your advantage, review the problems you're facing, as well as any information you're trying to encode into memory, before you head to bed. Your mind will continue processing these things while you rest.

4. Step back.

If you followed the tactics in the first half of the book—and especially if you've started to meditate—chances are the size of your attentional space has expanded. As this happens, it becomes increasingly important that you enter scatterfocus mode in order to *intentionally* scatter your attention.

Research suggests that the larger your attentional space, the more likely you are to continue stubbornly hammering away at complex tasks on which you're stuck. This is where scatterfocus trounces hyperfocus—scatterfocus is much better at piecing together solutions to complex, nonlinear problems. The better you're able to focus, the less prone you are to mind wandering and the more important it is that you purposefully *un*focus.

It's also worth taking your time in solving the problems presented by creative tasks. Purposefully delaying creative decisions—as long as you don't face an impending deadline—lets you continue to make potentially more valuable connections. For example, the longer you wait before sending an important email response, the better and more articulate your reply is likely to be. The same is true for tasks like deciding between a few potential hires, brainstorming a revamped design for your company's logo, or outlining a course you're teaching.

5. Intentionally leave tasks unfinished.

The more abruptly you stop working on a creative task, the more you'll think about it when you switch to another. Leave some residue in your attentional space for your mind to continue processing the initial task. For example, try stopping work on a complicated report midway through a sentence.

Leaving tasks partly completed helps you keep them front of mind as you encounter external and internal solution cues.

6. Consume more valuable dots.

We are what we consume. You can take deeper advantage of scatterfocus mode when you become deliberate about the information you take in. Consuming new dots exposes a wealth of new information and triggers that you can use to solve complex problems.

I've devoted the next chapter to exploring this idea. These dots have an enormous effect on what we focus on, can make or break our creativity and productivity, and are the lens through which we view the world.

CHAPTER 9

COLLECTING DOTS

CLUSTERING

Unresolved problems aren't the only things that sit at the front of our minds. All of the other dots we've accumulated matter just as much, if not more. This knowledge is what helps us become more creative in scatterfocus mode: the more valuable the dots we collect, the more we have to connect.

In practice, the dots we consume and connect are so important because our focus is always filtered through what we already know. Gazing at the ocean, a biologist might ponder all the creatures that lurk beneath its surface, an artist might consider the colors she'd use to paint it, a sailor might take note of the condition of the wind and the waves, while a writer might try to think about the words he'd use to describe it.

People become experts on particular subjects by accumulating and connecting enough dots related to them, in the form of experiences, knowledge, and best practices. Our brains are naturally programmed to cluster related dots. As a simple example, think back to when you first learned to write. You likely began by learning the letters of the alphabet—how they were shaped, what they sounded like, and so on. These were the first dots you accumulated on the topic:

d, s, c, h, s . . .

At this point your brain started connecting these dots, clustering them into alphabetical order, distinguishing the consonants from the vowels, and learning how to pronounce different syllables:

doe, sa, ha, sh . . .

You then began clustering these dots further to form words. To process the new ideas more deeply, you likely connected them to various pictures, as well as to objects in the world around you:

dog, sat, cup, seven, had, shatter . . .

After this point, you began clustering words and concepts together into phrases, sentences, and paragraphs:

The dog sat on the shattered cup and had to get seven stitches.

As you read this book, your knowledge of phrases, sentences, and paragraphs is so embedded in your mind that the act of reading has become implicit: you no longer have to think about it.

Reading is a compelling example of the power of collecting and connecting dots. By learning something new, you transfer dots from your external environment to your memory so you can link them and make use of them later. From the moment you're born to the day you die, your brain is always engaged in this process.

As we cluster more and more dots about a given topic, we naturally develop expertise, which in turn helps us better manage our attentional space. Curiously, the more we know about a subject, the less attentional space that information consumes. Recall that our attentional space can hold around four chunks of information at once. The more dots we're able to cluster, the more efficiently we're able to use that space, as we can accommodate and process a lot more pieces of information when they're linked together. We read more efficiently by processing words and sentences than by processing individual letters. An expert pianist can process all the elements of a piece of music—the melody, harmony, tempo, and so on—better than someone who has been playing for only a few weeks, which means she can make more efficient use of her attentional space, and maybe even daydream while she plays.

We do the same by collecting more dots related to our own work and investing in building relevant knowledge and skills. This lets us make more efficient use of our attentional space, whether we're using that accumulated information to hyperfocus on a task or piecing together new ideas in scatterfocus mode. We can work with more expertise and creativity because we've already done the due diligence to cluster this information together.*

Working with more information at our disposal also helps us make more intuitive decisions, because we're able to subconsciously summon preexisting knowledge in our memories. This information prompts us to respond appropriately in a situation, even if we're not consciously aware that we're doing so. For example, during a conversation we can intuit that a member of our team is upset and that there's something she's not telling us. We know this to be the case because we've experienced the same situation in the past and, on some level, remember the signs that indicated that she was unsettled. This is how intuition works: it's the process of acting on information we remember but don't consciously retrieve.

We are what we pay attention to, and almost nothing influences our productivity and creativity as much as the information we've consumed in the past. Accumulating many valuable dots helps us in innumerable ways. We become able to connect our challenges with the

---

* If you've ever felt like a fraud or an impostor in your field, you're not alone. The next time you do, simply consider how many dots you've accumulated and connected about a given topic relative to everyone else. Chances are you understand the nuances and complexity of the topic just as much as whomever you're comparing yourself with.

lessons we've learned. Our scatterfocus episodes become more productive as we link valuable ideas, especially as we become more responsive to new insight triggers by exposing ourselves to new dots. And our hyperfocus episodes become more productive, since we're able to make more efficient use of our attentional space, avoid mistakes, see opportunities for shortcuts, make better high-level decisions, and approach our work with more knowledge in hand.*

THE VALUE OF A DOT

Just as there are limits to how well we're able to focus, the same can be said about how much information we can collect. While our brain has nearly limitless storage space, our attention is far more restricted. Getting information into our brain is akin to filling an Olympic-sized swimming pool with a garden hose. While we're able to hold a huge amount, we can fill it up only gradually.

This makes it essential that we deliberately consume dots.

No two pieces of information are created equal. Consuming a book or having an engaging conversation with someone smarter than you will enable you to collect more valuable dots than doing something like watching TV or reading a gossip magazine. This is not to say that consuming popular culture isn't fun—life would suck without the occasional Netflix binge. And you'd probably get more than a little bored if you spent every spare minute reading dense books and academic journals.

---

* Through this lens, intelligence and creativity are very similar constructs. Both intelligence and creativity involve connecting dots, but in different ways. Intelligence involves connecting dots so we understand a given topic more intricately. Creativity also involves connecting dots—but in new and novel ways. Seen this way, intelligence and creativity aren't something we're born with—they're something we earn as we collect and connect enough dots about a given topic.

At the same time, it's worth auditing and increasing the quality of dots you consume regularly. The most creative and productive people defend their attentional space religiously, allowing only the most valuable dots to be encoded.

So how do you measure the value of a dot?

First, the most valuable dots are both useful and entertaining—like a TED talk. Useful dots stay relevant for a long time and are also practical. Their entertainment value makes you more engaged as you consume them. While it's fairly easy to tell if something's entertaining, there are several ways to measure how useful it is.

Useful information is typically actionable and helps you reach your goals. For example, listening to a few talking heads argue about political issues on TV probably isn't actionable *or* conducive to your personal goals. It also sucks up time that you'd otherwise spend consuming more important dots.

Reading a science book or a biography about a historical figure is much more valuable. Works like these can inspire you with a new perspective, are (relatively) practical, are nonspeculative, and can help you reach your personal goals in the short and long term. The information they contain also has a longer shelf life.

As well as being actionable and beneficial, useful dots are also either related to what you've consumed in the past or *completely unrelated* to what you already know.

Consuming information adjacent to what you've taken in before allows you to develop a constellation of dots around a single idea. If you're a software engineer, taking a course to learn a new programming language or reading a book on managing engineers is obviously a productive use of your time, attention, and energy. Any piece of information that supports your existing skills is a good use of time. The more expansive your constellation of dots, the more valuable connections you're able to make. Your brain even releases more dopamine, a pleasure chemical, when you consume information that supports what you know.

At the same time, it's also immensely valuable to consume dots that are *unrelated* to what you know. Taking in novel data gives you an opportunity to question whether you're consuming only information that confirms your existing beliefs, and it may provide an insight trigger. Again, your brain is attracted to and wired to remember novel information.

If you're in doubt about consuming something, ask yourself: How do you think your life will be different knowing this piece of information? The tactics in this book are all intended to help you manage your attention deliberately. The same principle applies here—when your creativity is effectively the sum of the dots you connect, consuming information on autopilot mode is one of the least useful activities to engage in.

COLLECTING MORE VALUABLE DOTS

Generally speaking, practicality does not always equal entertainment:

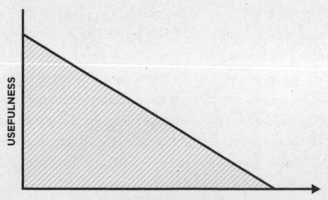

This isn't always the case—you may, for example, find some serious books more entertaining than reality TV shows—but most of what you consume will follow this trend.

We can further separate the most useful things we consume from the least useful:

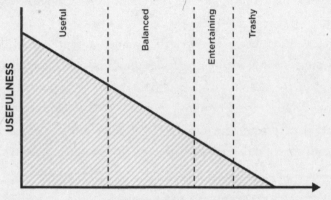

On the left side of this chart are the most **useful** dots we consume. This information is actionable, is accurate, helps us reach our goals, and remains relevant for a long time. It may also be related to what we already know—so it allows us to connect and cluster more valuable dots—or unrelated to what we know, leading to more serendipitous connections. For me, things like nonfiction books, online courses, and journal articles about productivity are in this category.

Useful information is typically the densest of the three categories. Books are a good illustration: while a book can sometimes take less than ten hours to read, it can take *decades* to write and may contain a lifetime of lessons that the author has learned and summarized. Books provide access to the highest-quality thinking and most useful dots on pretty much any topic.

Having an unlimited amount of energy to consume useful information throughout the day would be ideal, but this obviously isn't possible, even if we frequently replenish our supply of mental energy. However powerful our brains are as dot-connecting machines, consuming exclusively nonentertaining material can quickly become a chore. That's why it's also important to seek out **balanced** dots—information that is both useful *and* entertaining. Countless things fit into this category, including novels, podcasts, documentaries, and TED talks. The entertainment value of this information makes it easier to become engrossed in it, and as a result, we're more likely to continue consuming it and become actively involved with the information it provides.

Finally, there's the bottom third of what we consume: information that's **entertaining** or, at worst, **trashy**. Though, like junk food, it can be fun to consume in the moment, this information is the least dense, isn't practical, and won't help you live your life or reach your goals. This category includes the TV shows we binge-watch, the mindless books we read, and most social media websites. We usually consume this material passively on autopilot mode. While some of it is genuinely entertaining—the top 50 percent or so—the bottom half is trash information and is usually some combination of novel, pleasurable, and threatening, characteristics that make it easy to crave.

As a rule, we should

- consume more **useful** information, especially when we have the energy to process something more dense;
- consume **balanced** information when we have less energy;
- consume **entertaining** information with intention or when we're running low on energy and need to recharge; and
- consume less **trashy** information.

There are two steps to upping the quality of information you collect:

1. Take stock of everything you consume.
2. Intentionally consume more valuable information.

The purpose of consuming more valuable dots isn't to turn you into a Vulcan automaton who consumes only worthwhile information in your spare time. Where's the fun in that? The point is to let you step back from the information you do consume so you can determine with more intentionality what to take in. It's impossible to become more productive or creative without first reflecting on your work and life—this is what makes tactics like defining your most productive tasks, setting intentions, and letting your mind wander so powerful. Defining your most valuable dots is just another of these tactics.

To begin your audit, assign everything that you consume to one of the four categories of information: useful, balanced, entertaining, and trashy. Include the apps you fire up automatically, the websites you routinely visit, the books you read in your spare time, the shows and movies you watch on TV and Netflix, and any other relevant information you take in. It can be helpful to carry a notepad for a few days to list everything you consume (and, if you want, for how long you consume it). Do this at home and at work. If you consume a lot of books, courses, and other information for your job, it can be helpful to make two lists: one for the things you consume professionally and another for what you consume for personal benefit or pleasure.

You'll likely notice immediately a few things you want to change— the amount of time you spend on social media apps, reading news websites, or watching TV. You may also find patterns that surprise you. For example, the average American consumes thirty-four hours of TV a week. If you're one of them, that's a lot of time you could be spending on more useful pursuits. You may also notice what you're lacking—such as the fact that you don't read any fiction, even though you've always enjoyed it, or that it's been awhile since you invested in learning a new hobby.

Once you've taken stock, here are ten ideas for how you can change your habits to intentionally consume more valuable information. Start by trying two or three that resonate particularly strongly with you.

1. Consume things you care about, especially when few others do.

When listing the information you take in, you may have found you enjoy consuming things that other people tend to underappreciate or shy away from.

Maybe you love taking coding courses in your spare time—an activity that may feel like a chore for most people. Or you love listening to audiobooks about productivity (I plead guilty).

Double down on developing the skills and knowledge that *you* find entertaining. Also opt for the *medium* you prefer—if you learn best by listening, try consuming audiobooks instead of physical books; if you prefer visuals, try watching TED talks instead of listening to an audiobook.

2. Eliminate some trash.

Passively consuming pointless trash adds nothing to your life. Choose two items that don't bring you genuine enjoyment, and eliminate them entirely. Look out for material that, while stimulating in the moment, doesn't leave you satisfied afterward. Be ruthless in defending your attention. Every time you stop consuming trash, you make room for something useful to add value to your life.

3. Choose a few valuable things to *add*.

What useful books can you read, courses can you take, or conversations can you have that might prove useful later? Can you consume more complex information about a certain topic to take your expertise to the next level? What about yourself have you been wanting to improve, or what have been eager to know more about at work or at home?

Add something valuable for each worthless thing you eliminate. Push yourself: the most valuable information you can consume is material that challenges you and usually requires your full attention.

4. Notice what you consume on autopilot mode.

Pay special attention to what you pursue when you're low on energy or as you transition from one task to another. Often these objects of attention are just convenient and don't add much value to your life.

When a friend you're dining with leaves the table for a few minutes, what apps do you mindlessly open on your phone? Do you reach for your phone as soon as you wake up? What sites do you visit when you're surfing the internet on autopilot?

5. Veg out . . . intentionally.

You're perfectly productive whenever you accomplish what you intend to. This is true whether your goal is to read a chapter of a textbook or watch four episodes of *Game of Thrones*.

If you're going to veg out, do so with intention—set the criteria for what you plan to do, such as the number of episodes you'll get through, what you'll eat as you watch, what you'll do afterward, and so on. This not only allows you to act with intention but also leaves you feeling less guilty so that you actually *enjoy* yourself.

6. Reevaluate what you're consuming
as you're consuming it.

In addition to being more selective about what you consume, you should reevaluate content *as* you consume it—skipping or skimming anything that's not worth your time. The Zeigarnik effect makes us want to finish what we start, but every minute we spend on something useless is a minute we lose working on something useful.

After you begin a book, movie, or TV series, assess along the way whether you should pursue it to the end.

7. Get things to *bid* for your attention.

View the descriptions of podcasts, TV shows, movies, and books as a pitch for your time and attention.

You don't have to listen to every podcast that automatically downloads, every show your DVR records, or every book a friend recommends. Deciding whether something merits your attention takes an extra step, but it's a decision that will save hours you can then devote to something better.

8. In the moment, zoom out.

Try zooming out to a larger time frame if you're having trouble deciding in the moment between a few different things to consume.

If you spend any time on social media sites, you may be familiar with those oddly satisfying cooking videos that show an entire meal being made in half a minute. Spinach is reduced to one fifth its size in a second, and small chunks of chicken cook in two seconds. You can zoom out on the material you're considering consuming in a similar way. Let's say you find yourself with an hour to spend however you want. Take a step back to observe your life from afar. How would you want to see yourself occupying that time if it were sped up into a thirty-second video?

Would you want to see yourself lying like a blob on the couch watching *Sherlock* on Netflix or mindlessly tapping on your tablet? Or would you rather watch a video of yourself poring over a hundred pages of a book? Zooming out to observe the impacts of your actions will nudge you to consume more valuable information.

9. Invest in serendipity.

Consume challenging things outside the boundaries of your expertise, ones that force you to make more disparate connections. The more disparate the dots you connect, the more valuable the connections often end up being.

Set your browser's homepage to open with Wikipedia's "random article" bookmark. Look through the AMA (Ask Me Anything) section on Reddit, where world-renowned experts answer popular questions from everyday people. Go see a band you've never heard of. Read a book on a topic you know nothing about. Take a class in a subject you've always been curious about—like quilting, dancing, or public speaking. Pick up a biography about a historical figure whose name you know but whose life story you don't. I signed up for an online course on coding iPhone apps several few months back. Today it's one of my favorite things to do in my spare time.

10. Double down on what's valuable.

There are some topics you know more about, and some things you're better at, than almost anyone in the world. The more dots you collect around these particular topics or skills, the more of an expert you'll become.

For each worthless thing you eliminate, consider doubling down on something you're already good at or a subject you know a lot about. If you're a teacher, for example, instead of firing up Netflix on autopilot mode after work, consider taking a course to invest in new professional skills. When you double down on what you're already accomplished at, you'll be surprised by how much more productive and creative you become.

LIKE MAGIC

As we continue to assemble a constellation of dots around a certain topic, ideas begin to build upon one another. Eventually ideas become magic.

I love this quote from British science fiction writer Arthur C. Clarke: "Any sufficiently advanced technology is indistinguishable from magic." I'd take this a step further to argue that any sufficiently complex *decision* or *idea* is also indistinguishable from magic. Whenever we don't understand the complex network of dots that contribute to some result, we ascribe it to magic or genius.

I've had an obsession with magic tricks since I can remember, but I find figuring out the workings behind a complex illusion far more satisfying than seeing the trick itself. Illusions stop being magical the moment you discover how they're done—but learning how they're done feels like a eureka moment in and of itself, as a set of jumbled puzzle pieces locks into place.

Like a magician's, the methods of a genius are mysterious—until you untangle the web of connections that leads to them. These individuals usually have more experience, have put in more hours of deliberate practice, and, most important, have connected more dots than anyone else. As author Malcolm Gladwell wrote: "Practice isn't the thing you do once you're good. It's the thing you do that makes you good."

Albert Einstein was undoubtedly a genius—he connected more dots, in more unique ways, than almost any other human. At the same time, he was bound by the same mental limits that we all are. To conceive of an idea like the general theory of relativity, he had to collect and connect an incredible number of dots so he could bridge ideas from nature and mathematical concepts, forming connections others hadn't. To let his mind wander habitually, he played the violin for hours on end.* Einstein *worked* to attain his genius. As he put it, "I have no special talents, I am only passionately curious." Asking questions like "What would it be like to race alongside a light beam?" he spun complex webs of dots to formulate his theory of relativity. Despite his accomplishments, even Einstein was afflicted with imposter syndrome, once telling his wife, Elsa, while listening to the cheers of a thousand people outside his hotel room, "I'm afraid we're swindlers. We'll end up in prison yet."

While we often find the story of a lone, driven genius compelling, all geniuses have put in time and effort to achieve greatness. That includes Mozart, who wrote his first symphony at the age of eight. Daniel Levitin, the author of *This Is Your Brain on Music*, proposed a theory to account for Mozart's musical genius. "We don't know how much Mozart practiced," Levitin writes, "but if he started at age two and worked thirty-two hours a week (quite possible, given his father's reputation as a stern taskmaster) he would have made his first 10,000 hours by the age of eight." The "ten-thousand-hour rule" is a popular one—

---

* There are countless examples of others who let their mind wander to connect ideas. To write *Hamilton*, arguably the best Broadway show ever created, composer Lin-Manuel Miranda would make musical loops in a computer program and then walk around in scatterfocus mode until the lyrics came to him.

it's the length of effortful practice, some suggest, that it takes to acquire an expert level of performance at a certain skill. While the rule doesn't apply in every case—you could probably become a world-class master chocolate bar eater in less time—it's a fairly reliable yardstick. Ten thousand hours is enough time to build a rich constellation of dots around a certain topic or skill.

MAKING SCATTERFOCUS A HABIT

I hope that by now I've sold you on the remarkable benefits of scatterfocus mode. Scatterfocus lets you find useful connections between disparate ideas and experiences, recharge, and plan for the future. To reap these benefits, you simply have to let your mind rest and wander—preferably while doing something habitual.

How frequently you should scatter your attention will depend on a host of factors. For one, it will be tied to how often you use (and need to recharge) your ability to hyperfocus. Hyperfocus consumes mental energy, while scatterfocus is energy restorative.

Scattering your attention will be particularly beneficial when your work demands that you connect more complex, disparate ideas. For example, you should scatter your attention more often if you're a researcher responsible for designing experiments or a video game designer who constructs story lines. The more creativity your job requires, the more often you should scatter your attention. In most cases, the knowledge work of today benefits from as much creativity as we can bring to it.

Finally, the frequency with which you scatter your attention should reflect how important it is that you find the right approach to your work. Another of my favorite quotes is from Abraham Lincoln, who said, "Give me six hours to chop down a tree and I will spend the first four sharpening the axe." Whether we're planning a home renovation project, allocating our team's budget, or designing a research study, the approach we take to the task at hand matters. The more scatterfocus time we schedule as we're putting together a plan, the more time we'll save later.

The brain needs a few minutes to switch between hyperfocus and scatterfocus. Therefore, taking scatterfocus breaks that are at least fifteen minutes long will yield better results than trying to take advantage of tiny chunks of time throughout the day. But even brief breaks will help you become more creative, for while they may not leave sufficient time to piece together complex eureka insights, they'll definitely enable you to set intentions for what to do next, rest, and capture the open loops at the top of your mind. All three flavors of scatterfocus—habitual, capture, and problem-crunching—work in both small and large periods of time, though they'll provide you with more benefits at longer durations.

As well as entering scatterfocus mode on work breaks, there are countless other opportunities to apply scatterfocus during the day:

- Disconnect from the internet between 8:00 p.m. and 8:00 a.m.
- Notice when you finish a task, and use that as a cue to scatter your attention for a bit.
- Buy a cheap alarm clock so you're not immediately distracted by your phone when you wake up.
- Walk to get a coffee carrying only a notepad.
- As a challenge to yourself, leave your phone at home for an entire day.
- Take an extra-long shower.
- Make yourself bored for five minutes and notice what thoughts run through your head.
- Tame distractions and simplify your environment to make sure your attention doesn't overflow the next time you do a creative hobby.

- Cook with music playing instead of watching something enter-taining.
- Go for a nature walk.
- Visit an art gallery.
- Work out without music or a podcast.

Objectively speaking, scatterfocus might seem fairly unproductive. You're on a bus staring out the window. You're walking through nature or jogging without headphones. You're in a waiting room writing in a notepad instead of tapping on your phone. Though you don't look busy, your mind certainly is.

Scatterfocus is the most creative mode of your brain. Just as with hyperfocus, it's worth spending as much time as you possibly can prac-ticing it.

WORKING TOGETHER

BLENDING HYPERFOCUS AND SCATTERFOCUS

In many ways hyperfocus and scatterfocus are complete opposites. At any given moment, we're either doing something (with external attention) or thinking about something (with internal attention). We're unable to be in both hyperfocus mode and scatterfocus mode at the same time.

For all of the ways they differ, though, there are a lot of useful opportunities for the two modes to work together. When we focus, we consume and collect dots; when we scatter our attention, we connect these dots. Hyperfocusing allows us to remember more, which leads to more valuable connections made in scatterfocus mode. Scatterfocus lets us recharge, which in turn provides more energy to hyperfocus. The insights we unearth in scatterfocus help us work smarter later. In these ways and others, deliberately managing our attention is a practice with compounding benefits.

There are several strategies you can deploy that let you take greater advantage of both hyperfocus and scatterfocus. These strategies will help regardless of which mode you happen to be in.

INVEST IN YOUR HAPPINESS

If you wade through the many books, articles, and other works of research on the subject of happiness, you're likely to become depressed only by the sheer amount of advice that exists. Some of it is useful, but a lot of empty promises are also made.

It's important to make a distinction between legitimately investing in happiness and merely thinking more positively. To put it bluntly, positive thinking does not work to make you more happy or productive. In fact, research has shown it's *counter*productive. In one study, the more an overweight woman fantasized about being skinny, the less weight she lost over a year. In another, the more postsurgery patients fantasized about their recovery, the slower the improvement in their condition. In other studies, fantasizing positively about the future made participants perform worse on tests, decreased people's odds of entering new romantic relationships, prompted a lower mastery of everyday life, and even led people to contribute less to charity.

Positive thinking lets us feel successful in the moment, but at the price of making an actual plan to become successful later. In practice, there's little difference between positive thinking and wishful thinking.

What *does* work to increase our level of happiness? Spending time on things that boost our level of positive affect: how good we feel. There is a wealth of actual research demonstrating that becoming happier helps us manage our attention, as well as suggesting proven ways to boost our level of happiness. Curiously, the more we invest in our happiness, the more productive we become in hyperfocus mode and the more creative we become in scatterfocus mode.

Before getting into why, it's worth noting that you're likely to find yourself feeling happier simply by practicing the ideas in this book. You're significantly less content when your mind wanders against your will, even when it's wandering to neutral topics. You're about as happy when your mind is unintentionally wandering to a positive topic as you are when focusing on something mundane. Practicing hyperfocus and working with fewer distractions helps focus more attention on the present. *Intentionally* letting your mind wander takes the guilt, doubt, and stress out of the process, because you choose to unwind rather than doing so against your will. Generally speaking, a wandering mind makes us less happy, unless we're thinking about something we're interested in, something useful, or something novel. Scatterfocus—the intentional form of mind wandering—lets us experience all three.

Why, exactly, does investing in happiness foster productivity and creativity?

First, and most important, **a positive mood expands the size of your attentional space**, regardless of which mode you're in.

When you're happy, the amount of dopamine in the logical part of your brain rises, which leads you to approach your work with more energy and vigor—and because you have more attentional space to work with, you have the resources you need to focus more deeply and accomplish more. Being in a good mood also makes you better at recalling information on the fly. You also consume information more actively: the happier you are, the more likely you are to put ideas together in new and interesting ways, and the better you're able to overcome "functional fixedness" and, like MacGyver, see new uses for familiar things. Happiness also encourages you to seek more variety—but not the risky kind.

On the other hand, **a negative mood shrinks the size of your attentional space**. Unhappy people are less productive—full stop. The less happy you are, the more often your mind wanders against your will, and the less attention you bring to what's in front of you. The less happy you feel, the more important it is to tame distractions, as you have less attentional space and energy to resist them. The places where your mind wanders are also different when you're feeling negative—you're more likely to make your way to the distant past, ruminating on events that took place then.* While you can sometimes benefit from reliving past experiences, in the short run your productivity suffers—when your mind wanders more to the past, you plan for the future less often and assemble fewer productive ideas. And at the same time that your unwanted mind-wandering episodes increase, they become less pleasant and productive. This is why it's so important to capture the problems you're tackling when in a negative mood: whenever you're feeling miserable, you're often also dealing with a number of serious issues. The Zeigarnik effect—which keeps unresolved problems front of mind—forces you to think of them more.

People who are unhappy also take longer to refocus after an interruption and dwell more often on their failures. According to one study, habits that train our brain to wander less—such as mindfulness and meditation—are even "effective in reducing relapse in recovering depressive individuals."

While there is little research on exactly to what degree your attentional space expands when you're happy, happiness expert and Harvard-trained psychologist Shawn Achor found that happier people are 31 percent more productive than those in a negative or neutral state. Happiness also helps you become more creative in scatterfocus mode. You're more likely to experience insightful solutions to problems when you're in a positive frame of mind, which is not surprising, given that your brain has more attentional space and energy with which to work.

---

* The way researchers measured this in a lab was by having participants listen to either happy or mournful music while saying either positive or negative statements. Some participants heard uplifting music like Mozart's *Eine kleine Nachtmusik* while uttering statements like "I have complete confidence in myself." Others listened to sadder music like Barber's *Adagio for Strings* while uttering statements like "Just when I think things are going to get better, something else goes wrong."

How, then, can we invest in our happiness using the findings of science?

One of my favorite studies—the same one that discovered that we spend 47 percent of our time daydreaming—sampled thousands of participants throughout the day, asking two questions: what were the subjects doing at the instant they were sampled (participants received a notification on their phones), and how happy did they feel doing that thing? At the time of the study's publication, the researchers had received more than 250,000 responses from thousands of subjects. Here are the top five activities that made them the happiest:

5. Listening to music
4. Playing
3. Talking and investing in their relationships
2. Exercising
1. Making love

It's worth noting that our minds wander the least when we're making love—and that we're significantly happier doing so than we are doing anything else. Nothing else comes close. (To *really* invest in your attention, try doing all five things at once.)

As well as these activities, there are a number of other habits that have been proven to make people happier. One of my favorite researchers in the happiness field is the aforementioned Shawn Achor, the author of *The Happiness Advantage*. In the book, and in his TED talk, Shawn offers a few science-backed strategies to bolster your happiness. A few of his top suggestions:

• Recalling three things you're grateful for at the end of each day (a good companion tactic to the Rule of 3, discussed in chapter 3)

- Journaling at the end of each day about one good experience you had
- Meditating (see chapter 5)
- Performing a random act of kindness

While moods and attitudes aren't necessarily dots and ideas you can focus on and remember, they do greatly influence how you perceive and relate to what's in your attentional space, and they affect the size of your attentional space itself. Happiness is the rose-colored lens we place atop our attentional space, which allows us to relate to our experiences in a more productive and creative fashion.

If you need a boost, pick a few items from each of these lists to try. Reflect on the difference they make for you. Try all nine ideas, and keep what works. At the end of the day, these strategies won't only make you happier—they'll also make you more productive and creative.

WORK AROUND YOUR ENERGY LEVELS

As you've probably experienced, energy levels over the course of the day are anything but constant. They fluctuate according to when your body is programmed to have the most energy (e.g., if you happen to be an early bird or a night owl), how often you exercise, what you eat, and whether you get enough sleep.

Like energy levels, your focus and productivity aren't consistent either. You're the most productive when you dedicate your energy-rich moments to your most complex, meaningful tasks.

If you've read my previous book, *The Productivity Project*, you're already familiar with this idea. Hyperfocus is most effective during your peak energy times—I call these your Biological Prime Time (BPT), and the precise times of day differ for everyone. (By charting your energy levels for a week or two, you'll be able to identify your own patterns.) The more productive tasks you do during your BPT, the more productive you become.

There's a flip side to this concept when it comes to scatterfocus. Scatterfocus is most powerful when you have the *least* energy. Your brain is less inhibited during these periods and doesn't hold back the ideas it generates. Analytic problems require focused attention to solve, but solutions to creative problems come when you connect the greatest number of ideas. One study discovered we solve *27.3 percent* more insight problems during our nonoptimal time of day, when we're naturally more tired.

I call these time periods when we have the least energy our Creative Prime Time.

There's no shortage of research examining when we naturally have the most energy. For most people this occurs during the late morning (around 11:00 a.m.) and midafternoon (around 2:00 or 3:00 p.m.). Our energy is typically lowest right after lunch.

Energy levels also fluctuate throughout the week: we're typically the least engaged with our work on Mondays, when we experience the most boredom, and are the most engaged on Fridays.* Everyone is different, of course: if you're an early bird who springs out of bed at 5:00 a.m., your prime time might fall earlier in the day, and afternoons might be the best time for creative work. Similarly, night owls may find they're most productive when others have long since gone to bed.

A great way to work smarter is to schedule tasks that require focused

---

* Another random, fun finding from this study: we do the greatest number of rote tasks on Thursdays (about a third of the routine tasks we do throughout the entire week). If you find you fall into this pattern, it might be worth seeing Thursdays as your "Maintenance Day"—when you do all the tasks you'd rather not focus on during the rest of the week.

attention during your BPT and tasks that require more creativity during your CPT. Block time for these tasks in your calendar.

DRINK ALCOHOL AND CAFFEINE STRATEGICALLY

As far as decreasing your inhibitions is concerned, you're probably familiar with the effects of alcohol. Much like being tired, drinking has been shown to make people better at solving creative problems. (To test this theory, I rewrote some of this chapter while sipping vodka sodas with a lime twist. I'll let you be the judge of whether it's any better than the others.)

A favorite study I encountered in writing this book was one that had participants get mildly intoxicated while watching the Disney/Pixar movie *Ratatouille*. The researchers split participants into two groups. One group was fed a bagel, as well as multiple vodka cranberry drinks—both in quantities relative to how much each participant weighed. The subjects consumed the drinks while watching the film. The second, significantly less lucky group also watched the movie but didn't consume any food or drinks in the process.

The study's findings were remarkable: after watching the movie, tipsy participants solved *38 percent* more creative word puzzles than the sober participants. Not only that, they solved the problems more quickly! (As you might have guessed, the drunk participants weren't better at solving logical problems.) Again, when it comes to solving creative problems, the less control we have over our attention, the better.

This is not intended to advocate the use of alcohol, which is, of course, not without its downsides. The *Ratatouille* study measured performance on tasks that required pure creativity, but most tasks require a mix of creativity *and* focus. When it comes time to focus on something, alcohol will absolutely obliterate your productivity.

If you're into meditation, experiment with having a drink or two before your next evening session. You'll experience this effect firsthand: consuming alcohol makes your mind wander more often while at the same time *decreasing* your meta-awareness. Alcohol affects two aspects of the quality of your attention: not only will you focus for a shorter period of time, but also it will take you longer to realize that your mind has wandered.

Being under the influence also diminishes the size of your attentional space and makes it difficult to focus on pretty much anything. The more you drink, the more your mind wanders, the less awareness you have to halt it, and the smaller your attentional space becomes. It's no wonder we remember less when we've had a few drinks—it's impossible to remember what we don't pay attention to in the first place.

In practice, alcohol is worth consuming only for very select tasks. If it's the end of the day and you want to brainstorm, sipping a wobbly pop will help. But keep in mind that it helps precisely because it decreases how much control you have over your attention.

I view drinking alcohol as a way by which we borrow energy and happiness from the following day. Sometimes this price is worth paying—such as when you're hanging out with friends you haven't seen in a long time—but often it simply isn't. If you drink alcohol, do so strategically: in those rare times when you want to let your mind roam more freely (and have nothing important planned afterward) or you want to steal some happiness from tomorrow.

Caffeine is another drug to consider consuming strategically. When it comes to managing attention, caffeine has the polar opposite effect of alcohol: while alcohol helps us scatterfocus, caffeine helps us hyperfocus.

The research is conclusive: caffeine boosts mental (and physical) performance in pretty much every measurable way:

- **It deepens our focus**, regardless of whether a task is simple or complex, and narrows it, which makes hyperfocusing on a task easier (but scatterfocus more difficult).

- **It helps us persevere**, especially with tasks that are long and tedious. (It boosts our determination regardless of how tired or fatigued we are.)

- **It improves our performance** on tasks that require verbal memory, a quick reaction time, or visuospatial reasoning (e.g., putting together a jigsaw puzzle).

In general, these effects diminish after the consumption of approximately 200 milligrams of caffeine (a single cup of coffee contains around 125 milligrams). Amounts greater than 400 milligrams should be avoided, as at that amount you begin to feel more anxious, and your performance becomes impaired. Again, take this advice only if you find it holds true for you. We all react differently to caffeine. Some metabolize it quickly and have a high tolerance, and others find their entire body vibrating after just a few sips. As with most productivity advice, implementing individual tactics with an awareness of how well they actually work for you is key.

Caffeine can also boost your performance on physical work and exercise—it helps you perform in hot conditions, boosts strength-training performance, and increases your tolerance for pain during exercise.

Just like alcohol, caffeine is not without its drawbacks, even when you consume healthier caffeinated drinks that aren't loaded with sugar, like black tea, green tea, or matcha (my personal favorite). As your body metabolizes caffeine out of your system, your energy crashes, and your productivity dips. Caffeine can also disrupt your sleep, which can make you less productive the next day.

Because of these costs, choose caffeine when you'll actually benefit from the mental or physical performance boost. Provided it's not too late in the day, consume a bit of caffeine the next time you're about to hyperfocus on a task or hit the gym for a big workout.* Instead of having a cup of coffee after you awake, wait until you get to work so you'll benefit from the boost when you work on your most productive tasks. If you have a brainstorming meeting first thing in the morning, consume caffeine *after* the session, keeping the walls of your attentional space low to let more ideas flow. If you have a pitch meeting, on the other hand, do the opposite.

OPEN OFFICES

I give productivity talks in many different workplaces, and over time I've noticed more companies adopting an open-office plan. Open offices are a mixed bag when it comes to focus and productivity.

It's easiest to focus when we work in an environment we can control, and obviously we have less control over our environment, and therefore our attention, in an open office. Research supports this: we distract ourselves *64 percent more often* in an open environment, and we're interrupted by others more often as well. An open office can seriously undermine your productivity if you do a lot of work that requires focused attention.

Open offices do have their benefits. One is that they support working for longer on a single project before switching to another. The

---

* If you're looking for a near-instantaneous boost, try caffeinated gum. Your body absorbs caffeine most quickly through the buccal tissue in your mouth.

reason for this is interesting: while our colleagues interrupt us more in an open environment, they're also more considerate about when they do. Because they can observe us working, they notice when we've reached a natural break point in our work—when we return to our desk after a meeting, at the end of a phone call, or when we stand up after completing something. In these environments we're interrupted more often when we're switching between tasks, so we don't need as much time and energy to refocus.

While this book focuses on personal productivity, our work doesn't exist in a vacuum: the projects on our plates are typically intertwined with the work of others. In highly collaborative work, the faster we can get information from others, and the more quickly they can get information from us, the better the collaboration, as the team will become more productive as a whole system.

The bottom line when it comes to open-office plans is that if the work you and your team does is hypercollaborative or involves a great deal of creativity and connecting ideas, an open office is probably worth its disadvantages. If your work involves a significant number of tasks that benefit from undisturbed focus, as more and more jobs seem to, an open office can be detrimental to your productivity.

If you're a manager, consider the type of work your team does before you plan for an open office. If you do decide this design is worth the potential productivity costs, be sure to educate your employees on how to manage interruptions. One study found that after a team understood how costly interruptions were, they fell by 30 percent.

It's also worth investigating whether most of the interruptions you (or your team) face come from a common source. For example, if you lead a group of programmers who are interrupted mostly for feature requests and questions about the product, create a tool for those outside your team to suggest new features, and produce more useful documentation, so the interruptions that do come in are less frequent and less costly. If you can't avoid adopting an open-office plan, be sure to designate a quiet zone where employees can hyperfocus without interruption.

CREATING A FOCUS RITUAL

By now we've covered how to integrate both hyperfocus and scatterfocus into your life and make a habit out of entering each mode daily.

Enter hyperfocus mode at least once a day to deal with your most productive tasks; eliminate distractions and concentrate on one important thing. Enter scatterfocus multiple times a day—particularly habitual scatterfocus mode—so that you can plan for the future, connect ideas, and recharge your ability to hyperfocus. Do the same at home, hyperfocusing on meaningful experiences and conversations and scatterfocusing when you need to plan, rest, or ideate.

Some weeks you may find that you need more of one than the other. One of my favorite weekly routines is a focus ritual, which I schedule for every Sunday evening or Monday morning to plan my week. During it I decide on my three weekly intentions and assess how much I'll need to hyperfocus and scatterfocus in the days ahead. I'd be lying if I said I spent a *lot* of time planning how long I'll dedicate to each mode—no one should do that. But I do consider, briefly, whether my week will benefit from one mode more than the other.

When doing the same for your own schedule, ask yourself questions like these:

- How much productivity and creativity will I need this week? Does an upcoming deadline mean I need to hyperfocus more than usual? Or do I have more space to plan for the future and connect ideas?

- What commitments do I have coming up that will get in the way of my hyperfocus and scatterfocus time (e.g., travel, a draining conference, or an inordinate number of meetings)? How can I deal with these obstacles in advance?

- How many blocks of time can I commit to hyperfocus and scatterfocus? Can I commit to these periods in my calendar?

NOTICING

This final chapter has explored a variety of ideas that will enable you to take even greater advantage of your attention. By investing in your happiness, working around your energy levels, drinking alcohol and caffeine strategically, considering your office environment, and taking into account both hyperfocus and scatterfocus as you plan your week, you'll be able to take deliberate management of your attention to the next level.

It's also important not to lose sight of one final concept that's paramount to managing attention well: awareness.

As you become more aware of what's occupying your attentional space, how much energy you have, and how full your attentional space is, you'll become more agile and adjust as conditions change. For example, if you've reached an impasse with a problem, awareness will give you the ability to determine whether the problem is more analytical or requires creative insight to solve—you can then enter hyperfocus or scatterfocus accordingly.

One of the best strategies to train your brain to become more aware is the hourly awareness chime I discussed in chapter 3. When the chime dings, reflect on what's occupying your attentional space, as well as the state of your attention. Odds are you haven't experimented with every idea in this book, but if you haven't already, do try this one. In addition to an hourly awareness chime, try picking a few cues you encounter each day, at work and at home, to use as reminders to check your attentional space.

Awareness is the thread that winds its way through most of the tactics in this book. When you're aware of what has taken hold of your attention, you're able to direct it back toward more important and meaningful things. You'll then work with greater purpose, focus for longer, and daydream less—all of which will increase the quality of your attention and the quality of your life.

Awareness is really just a process of noticing things, and there is a lot to notice. I hope you've discovered some of the curious ways your own attention works. Maybe you've noticed the quality of your attention: how much of your time you spend intentionally, the duration of your focus, and how long your mind wanders before you catch it doing so. Maybe you've noticed just how often you automatically pay attention to anything that's novel, pleasurable, or threatening. Maybe you've noticed how quickly objects of attention pass through your attentional space.

Above all, I hope you've become more productive, creative, and purpose-driven.

THE POWER OF MANAGING YOUR ATTENTION WELL

The benefits of effectively managing your attention are innumerable.

For starters, you feel more in control as you turn off autopilot mode and manage your attention deliberately. You begin to understand its limits and become better able to work within them—learning when you can and can't multitask. Your life becomes more meaningful, because you pay greater attention to meaningful experiences and process them more deeply. In this way, meaning isn't something we try to find—it's something we make an effort to *notice*. You get more done, because you're actually able to focus on important matters. You're able to think more clearly and become more engaged with your work. You plan for the future and set intentions more frequently. You feel better rested and less guilty about taking a step back. And you connect more ideas, while amassing constellations of them in your mind about topics that drive your curiosity further. This inspires you to become more creative, lets you work smarter and more intuitively, and makes you more productive on creative projects.

Hyperfocus can help you get an extraordinary amount done in a relatively short period of time. Scatterfocus lets you connect ideas—which helps you unearth hidden insights, become more creative, plan for the future, and rest. Together they will enable you to work and live with purpose.

Your attention is the most powerful tool at your disposal to live and work with greater productivity, creativity, and purpose. Managing it well will enable you to spend more time and energy on your most purposeful tasks and to work more often with intention, focus for longer periods, and stumble into fewer unwanted daydreams.

I hope you spend it wisely.

ACKNOWLEDGMENTS

For a book like this to come into existence, dozens of people had to play a part. Their work, summed up, is likely greater than my own.

First, I have never met in person many of the people who made this book possible. They are the researchers whose shoulders I stood upon in assembling it. Thank you to all those whose work is tucked away in the Notes section and in the pages of this book. Thank you especially to Gloria Mark, Mary Czerwinski, and Shamsi Iqbal, all at Microsoft Research, for meeting with me in person not once, but *three* times. Thank you also to Jonathan Schooler, Jonathan Smallwood, Peter Gollwitzer, and Sophie Leroy for so generously agreeing to chat.

Lucinda Blumenfeld, my literary agent, believed in the idea for this book from the very start and was once again the best partner anyone could ask for in publishing a book. Lucinda is one of those rare people who are never afraid to tell you what they think, but at the same time will always have your back. I'm thrilled I get to work with an agent as talented and generous as she is. Rick Kot, my editor extraordinaire at Viking, also believed in the idea of *Hyperfocus* from the very start and let me go wild with it. One of the best parts about writing this book was getting to work with Rick—truly one of the smartest, most talented, and kindest people I've met. (And I don't even need to suck up to him anymore, because he's already sent me his edits.) Thank you to Craig Pyette, my crazy-talented editor at Random House Canada, who so graciously provided editing notes that helped smooth the book out even further. Thank you also to Diego Núñez, Connor Eck, and Norma Barksdale, who provided invaluable support through the publishing process.

Thank you also to Hilary Duff and Victoria Klassen, who helped me research and edit this book. I have the tendency to write in a long-winded way, and Hilary trimmed literally thousands of words of chaff from this book. She gave you a couple hours of your life back, so you should probably thank her too. Victoria was, for a second time around, an extraordinary help in not just fact checking this book but also—as an especially big relief for me—formatting the Notes section, a task I wouldn't want to touch with a ten-foot pole. Thank you, Victoria!

In addition to those who helped shape this book, there are many others who played a part. Thank you to Hal Fessenden and Jennifer Choi for helping us find such fantastic publishers outside of the United States and Canada—including Robin Harvie at Macmillan in the United Kingdom. And to Carolyn Coleburn, Ben Petrone, Lydia Hirt, Nora Alice Demick and Alex McGill for helping share the idea of this book in the United States and Canada. Thank you also to Luise Jorgensen, whom I've had the pleasure of working with for more than four years now. I'm honestly not sure what I'd do without you, Luise (and that's not hyperbole).

Thank you to my readers, some of whom have been reading my work for many years. I hope you found this book worthy of your time and that this book, and my work that comes after it, pays dividends for you for many years to come.

And finally, thank you to Ardyn. Ardyn is my first reader, and I hope she always will be. I trust her more than anyone not only to strength-test my ideas but also to help me build them up in the first place. But much more important than anything work related, Ardyn is the love of my life who became my fiancée over the course of writing this book. Ardyn, from where I sit you're one of a kind. Thank you for turning me into somebody loved.

NOTES

CHAPTER 0: WHY FOCUS MATTERS

4n **how *interested* we are:** Shi Feng, Sidney D'Mello, and Arthur C. Graesser, "Mind Wandering While Reading Easy and Difficult Texts," *Psychonomic Bulletin & Review* 20, no. 3 (2013): 586–92.

5 **Studies show we can work:** Gloria Mark et al., "Neurotics Can't Focus: An *in situ* Study of Online Multitasking in the Workplace," in *Proceedings of the 2016 CHI Conference on Human Factors in Computing Systems* (New York: ACM, 2016), 1739–44, doi:10.1145/2858036.2858202.

CHAPTER 0.5: HOW TO BETTER FOCUS ON THIS BOOK

10 **coffee or tea:** David Mrazik, "Reconsidering Caffeine: An Awake and Alert New Look at America's Most Commonly Consumed Drug" (third-year paper, Harvard University, 2004), DASH: Digital Access to Scholarship at Harvard.

CHAPTER 1: SWITCHING OFF AUTOPILOT MODE

16 **require conscious deliberation:** Wendy Wood, Jeffrey Quinn, and Deborah Kashy, "Habits in Everyday Life: Thought, Emotion, and Action," *Journal of Personality and Social Psychology* 83, no. 6 (2002): 1281–97.

18n **before we do:** Erik D. Reichle, Andrew E. Reineberg, and Jonathan W. Schooler, "Eye Movements During Mindless Reading," *Psychological Science* 21, no. 9 (2010): 1300–1310.

CHAPTER 2: THE LIMITS OF YOUR ATTENTION

24 **experiences each second:** Timothy Wilson, *Strangers to Ourselves: Discovering the Adaptive Unconscious* (Cambridge, MA: Belknap Press, 2004).

24 **of our attention:** TED, "Mihaly Csikszentmihalyi: Flow, the Secret to Happiness," YouTube, October 24, 2008, www.youtube.com/watch?v=fXIeFJCqsPs.

25 **though, is four:** Nelson Cowan, "The Magical Mystery Four: How Is Working Memory Capacity Limited, and Why?" *Current Directions in Psychological Science* 19, no. 1 (2010): 51–57; Edward K. Vogel and Steven J. Luck, "The Capacity of Visual Working Memory for Features and Conjunctions," *Nature* 390, no. 6657 (1997): 279–81; Nelson Cowan, "The Magical Number 4 in Short-term Memory: A Reconsideration of Mental Storage Capacity," *Behavioral and Brain Sciences* 24, no. 1 (2001): 87–114.

27 **our conscious experiences:** Giorgio Marchetti, "Attention and Working Memory: Two Basic Mechanisms for Constructing Temporal Experiences," *Frontiers in Psychology* 5 (2014): 880.

27 **we need it:** Klaus Oberauer, "Design for a Working Memory," *Psychology of Learning and Motivation* 51 (2009): 45–100.

27n **chances at survival:** Ferris Jabr, "Does Thinking Really Hard Burn More Calories?" *Scientific American*, July 2012; Cowan, "Magical Mystery Four."

29 **"a short-term memory":** Marchetti, "Attention and Working Memory."

29 **watching a video:** Ibid.

29 **of the rest:** Shi Feng, Sidney D'Mello, and Arthur C. Graesser, "Mind Wandering While Reading Easy and Difficult Texts," *Psychonomic Bulletin & Review* 20, no. 3 (2013): 586–92.

30 *47 percent* **of the time:** Jonathan Smallwood and Jonathan W. Schooler, "The Science of Mind Wandering: Empirically Navigating the Stream of Consciousness," *Annual Review of Psychology* 66, no. 1 (2015): 487–518; Matthew A. Killingsworth and Daniel T. Gilbert, "A Wandering Mind Is an Unhappy Mind," *Science* 330, no. 6006 (2010): 932.

31 **minds had wandered:** Jonathan Smallwood, Merrill McSpadden, and Jonathan W. Schooler, "When Attention Matters: The Curious Incident of the Wandering Mind," *Memory & Cognition* 36, no. 6 (2008): 1144–50.

31 **mind is wandering:** Jennifer C. McVay, Michael J. Kane, and Thomas R. Kwapil, "Tracking the Train of Thought from the Laboratory into Everyday Life: An Experience-Sampling Study of Mind Wandering Across Controlled and Ecological Contexts," *Psychonomic Bulletin & Review* 16, no. 5 (2009): 857–63.

31 **just ten seconds:** Adam D. Baddeley, *Essentials of Human Memory* (Hove, UK: Psychology Press, 1999).

33 **same mental resources:** Daniel J. Levitin, "Why the Modern World Is Bad for Your Brain," *Guardian*, January 18, 2015.

41 **built-in "novelty bias":** Robert Knight and Marcia Grabowecky, "Prefrontal Cortex, Time, and Consciousness," *Knight Lab, Cognitive Neuroscience Research Lab*, 2000.

43 it into memory: Marchetti, "Attention and Working Memory."

44 the first place: Eyal Ophir et al., "Cognitive Control in Media Multitaskers," *Proceedings of the National Academy of Sciences of the United States of America* 106, no. 37 (2009): 15583–87.

45 interrupting us as well: Gloria Mark et al., "Neurotics Can't Focus: An *in situ* Study of Online Multitasking in the Workplace," in *Proceedings of the 2016 CHI Conference on Human Factors in Computing Systems* (New York: ACM, 2016), 1739–44, doi:10.1145/2858036.2858202.

45n before becoming distracted: Gloria Mark, Yiran Wang, and Melissa Niiya, "Stress and Multitasking in Everyday College Life: An Empirical Study of Online Activity," in *Proceedings of the SIGCHI Conference on Human Factors in Computing Systems* (New York: ACM 2014), 41–50, doi:10.1145/2556288.2557361.

46 transitioned to the next: Sophie Leroy, "Why Is It So Hard to Do My Work? The Challenge of Attention Residue When Switching Between Work Tasks," *Organizational Behavior and Human Decision Processes* 109, no. 2 (2009): 168–81.

47 ways to complete it: Ibid.

47 start to completion: Mark et al., "Neurotics Can't Focus."

49 before you catch it: Killingsworth and Gilbert, "A Wandering Mind Is an Unhappy Mind."

CHAPTER 3: THE POWER OF HYPERFOCUS

55 mistakes they made: Gordon D. Logan and Matthew J. C. Crump, "The Left Hand Doesn't Know What the Right Hand Is Doing: The Disruptive Effects of Attention to the Hands in Skilled Typewriting," *Psychological Science* 20, no. 10 (2009): 1296–300; Sian L. Beilock et al., "When Paying Attention Becomes Counterproductive: Impact of Divided Versus Skill-Focused Attention on Novice and Experienced Performance of Sensorimotor Skills," *Journal of Experimental Psychology: Applied* 8, no. 1 (2002): 6–16.

56 one thing intentionally: Shi Feng, Sidney D'Mello, and Arthur C. Graesser, "Mind Wandering While Reading Easy and Difficult Texts," *Psychonomic Bulletin & Review* 20, no. 3 (2013): 586–92.

56 our mind has wandered): Jonathan W. Schooler et al., "Meta-awareness, Perceptual Decoupling and the Wandering Mind," *Trends in Cognitive Sciences* 15, no. 7 (2011): 319–26.

56 object of attention: Wendy Hasenkamp et al., "Mind Wandering and Attention During Focused Meditation: A Fine-Grained Temporal Analysis of Fluctuating Cognitive States," *Neuroimage* 59, no. 1 (2012): 750–60.

58 47 percent of the day: Matthew A. Killingsworth and Daniel T. Gilbert, "A Wandering Mind Is an Unhappy Mind," *Science* 330, no. 6006 (2010): 932.

58 the original task: Gloria Mark, Victor Gonzalez, and Justin Harris, "No Task Left Behind? Examining the Nature of Fragmented Work," in *Proceedings of the SIGCHI*

Conference on Human Factors in Computing Systems (New York: ACM, 2005), 321–30, doi:10.1145/1054972.1055017.

63 **for doing so:** Claire M. Zedelius et al., "Motivating Meta-awareness of Mind Wandering: A Way to Catch the Mind in Flight?" *Consciousness and Cognition* 36 (2015): 44–53.

65 **by around 20 percent:** Peter M. Gollwitzer and Veronika Brandstätter, "Implementation Intentions and Effective Goal Pursuit," *Journal of Personality and Social Psychology* 73, no. 1 (1997): 186–99; Peter M. Gollwitzer, "Implementation Intentions: Strong Effects of Simple Plans," *American Psychologist* 54, no. 7 (1999): 493–503.

66 **odds of success:** Gollwitzer and Brandstätter, "Implementation Intentions and Effective Goal Pursuit," Gollwitzer, "Implementation Intentions: Strong Effects of Simple Plans."

67 **original goal automatically:** Gollwitzer and Brandstätter, "Implementation Intentions and Effective Goal Pursuit."

68 **do something simple:** Gollwitzer, "Implementation Intentions."

71 **rewarding or meaningful:** Allan Blunt, "Task Aversiveness and Procrastination: A Multi-dimensional Approach to Task Aversiveness Across Stages of Personal Projects" (master's thesis, Department of Psychology, Carleton University, 1998).

CHAPTER 4: TAMING DISTRACTIONS

74 **every *thirty-five* seconds:** Gloria Mark et al., "Neurotics Can't Focus: An *in situ* Study of Online Multitasking in the Workplace," in *Proceedings of the 2016 CHI Conference on Human Factors in Computing Systems* (New York: ACM, 2016), 1739–44, doi:10.1145/2858036.2858202.

74 **38 daily checks:** Gloria Mark et al., "Focused, Aroused, but So Distractible: Temporal Perspectives on Multitasking and Communications," in *Proceedings of the 18th ACM Conference on Computer Supported Cooperative Work & Social Computing* (New York: ACM, 2015), 903–916, doi:10.1145/2675133.2675221.

75 **stresses us out:** Gloria Mark, Daniela Gudith, and Ulrich Klocke, "The Cost of Interrupted Work: More Speed and Stress," in *Proceedings of the SIGCHI Conference on Human Factors in Computing Systems* (New York: ACM 2008), 107–110, doi:10.1145/1357054.1357072.

75 **about ten simultaneously:** Victor Gonzalez and Gloria Mark, "Constant, Constant, Multi-tasking Craziness: Managing Multiple Working Spheres," in *Proceedings of the SIGCHI Conference on Human Factors in Computing Systems* (New York: ACM, 2004), 599–606, doi:10.1145/985692.985707.

75 **before doing so:** Gloria Mark, Victor Gonzalez, and Justin Harris, "No Task Left Behind? Examining the Nature of Fragmented Work," in *Proceedings of the SIGCHI Conference on Human Factors in Computing Systems* (New York: ACM, 2005), 321–30, doi:10.1145/1054972.1055017.

75n **back on track:** Fiona McNab et al., "Age-Related Changes in Working Memory and the Ability to Ignore Distraction," *Proceedings of the National Academy of Sciences* 112, no. 20 (2015): 6515–18.

75n **distraction after another:** Leonard M. Giambra, "Task-Unrelated-Thought Frequency as a Function of Age: A Laboratory Study," *Psychology and Aging* 4, no. 2 (1989): 136–43.

75n **engaged in the workplace:** IORG Forum, "Rhythms of Attention, Focus and Mood with Digital Activity—Dr. Gloria Mark," YouTube, July 6, 2014, https://www.youtube.com/watch?v=0NUlFhxcVWc.

76n **have plummeted 17 percent:** Rani Molla, "How Apple's iPhone Changed the World: 10 Years in 10 Charts," *Recode*, June 2017.

77n **check your email:** Mark et al., "Focused, Aroused, but So Distractible."

80 **by someone else:** Mark, Gonzalez, and Harris, "No Task Left Behind?"; Ioanna Katidioti et al., "Interrupt Me: External Interruptions Are Less Disruptive Than Self-Interruptions," *Computers in Human Behavior* 63, (2016): 906–15.

80 **track more quickly:** Mark, Gudith, and Klocke, "Cost of Interrupted Work."

80n **come from others:** Mark, Gonzalez, and Harris, "No Task Left Behind?"; González and Mark, "Constant, Constant, Multi-tasking Craziness."

83 **out of your system:** David Mrazik, "Reconsidering Caffeine: An Awake and Alert New Look at America's Most Commonly Consumed Drug" (third-year paper, Harvard University, 2004), DASH: Digital Access to Scholarship at Harvard.

84 **ability to resist distractions:** Gloria Mark, Shamsi Iqbal, and Mary Czerwinski, "How Blocking Distractions Affects Workplace Focus and Productivity," in *Proceedings of the 2017 ACM International Joint Conference on Pervasive and Ubiquitous Computing and Proceedings of the 2017 ACM International Symposium on Wearable Computers* (New York: ACM Press, 2017), 928–34, doi:10.1145/3123024.3124558.

84 **periods of time:** Jennifer A. A. Lavoie and Timothy A. Pychyl, "Cyberslacking and the Procrastination Superhighway: A Web-Based Survey of Online Procrastination, Attitudes, and Emotion," *Social Science Computer Review* 19, no. 4 (2001): 431–44.

85 **yourself from distractions:** Mark, Iqbal, and Czerwinski, "How Blocking Distractions Affects Workplace Focus."

85 **correlated with procrastination:** John C. Loehlin and Nicholas G. Martin, "The Genetic Correlation Between Procrastination and Impulsivity," *Twin Research and Human Genetics: The Official Journal of the International Society for Twin Studies* 17, no. 6 (2014): 512–15.

86 **focus on your work:** John Trougakos and Ivona Hideg, "Momentary Work Recovery: The Role of Within-Day Work Breaks," in *Current Perspectives on Job-Stress Recovery*, vol. 7, *Research in Occupational Stress and Well-being*, ed. Sabine Sonnentag, Pamela L. Perrewé, and Daniel C. Ganster (West Yorkshire, UK: Emerald Group, 2009).

89 **early the night before:** Gloria Mark, Yiran Wang, and Melissa Niiya, "Stress and Multitasking in Everyday College Life: An Empirical Study of Online Activity," in

Proceedings of the SIGCHI Conference on Human Factors in Computing Systems (New York: ACM, 2014), 41–50, doi:10.1145/2556288.2557361.

93 **attention on email:** Ashish Gupta, Ramesh Sharda, and Robert A. Greve, "You've Got Email! Does It Really Matter to Process Emails Now or Later?" *Information Systems Frontiers* 13, no. 5 (2011): 637.

93 **span of a day:** Gloria Mark et al., "Focused, Aroused, but So Distractible: Temporal Perspectives on Multitasking and Communications," in *Proceedings of the 18th ACM Conference on Computer Supported Cooperative Work & Social Computing* (New York: ACM, 2015), 903–16, doi:10.1145/2675133.2675221.

94 **and reflexive way:** Thomas Jackson, Ray Dawson, and Darren Wilson, "Reducing the Effect of Email Interruptions on Employees," *International Journal of Information Management* 23, no. 1 (2003): 55–65.

94 **the forty-second mark:** Gupta, Sharda, and Greve, "You've Got Email!"

96 **peaceful and refreshing:** Gloria Mark, Stephen Voida, and Armand Cardello, "A Pace Not Dictated by Electrons: An Empirical Study of Work Without Email," in *Proceedings of the SIGCHI Conference on Human Factors in Computing Systems* (New York: ACM, 2012), 555–64, doi:10.1145/2207676.2207754.

96 **daily in meetings:** Infocom, "Meetings in America: A Study of Trends, Costs, and Attitudes Toward Business Travel and Teleconferencing, and Their Impact on Productivity" (Verizon Conferencing white paper).

97 **the modern office:** Chris Bailey, "The Five Habits of Happier, More Productive Workplaces" (Zipcar white paper, October 19, 2016).

100 **"compendium of information":** Shalini Misra et al., "The iPhone Effect: The Quality of In-Person Social Interactions in the Presence of Mobile Devices," *Environment and Behavior* 48, no. 2 (2016): 275–98.

101 **"connection, and relationship quality":** Andrew K. Przybylski and Netta Weinstein, "Can You Connect with Me Now? How the Presence of Mobile Communication Technology Influences Face-to-Face Conversation Quality," *Journal of Social and Personal Relationships* 30, no. 3 (2013): 237–46.

101n **conducive to creativity:** Kathleen D. Vohs, Joseph P. Redden, and Ryan Rahinel, "Physical Order Produces Healthy Choices, Generosity, and Conventionality, Whereas Disorder Produces Creativity," *Psychological Science* 24, no. 9 (2013): 1860–67.

101n **a walk, however:** Michael J. Larson, et al., "Cognitive and Typing Outcomes Measured Simultaneously with Slow Treadmill Walking or Sitting: Implications for Treadmill Desks," *PloS One* 10, no. 4 (2015): 1–13.

102n **we naturally have:** Shawn Achor, *The Happiness Advantage: The Seven Principles of Positive Psychology That Fuel Success and Performance at Work* (New York: Currency, 2010).

103 **not in cubicles:** Florence Williams, "This Is Your Brain on Nature," *National Geographic*, January 2016.

105 **it's relatively simple:** Morgan K. Ward, Joseph K. Goodman, and Julie R. Irwin, "The Same Old Song: The Power of Familiarity in Music Choice," *Marketing*

Letters 25, no. 1 (2014): 1–11; Agnes Si-Qi Chew et al., "The Effects of Familiarity and Language of Background Music on Working Memory and Language Tasks in Singapore," *Psychology of Music* 44, no. 6 (2016): 1431–38.

105n temperature for productivity: Greg Peverill-Conti, "Captivate Office Pulse Finds Summer Hours Are Bad for Business," *InkHouse for Captivate,* June 2012.

106 your attentional space: Lauren L. Emberson et al., "Overheard Cell-phone Conversations: When Less Speech Is More Distracting," *Psychological Science* 21, no. 10 (2010): 1383–88.

106n from a D to a B grade: Faria Sana, Tina Weston, and Nicholas J. Cepeda, "Laptop Multitasking Hinders Classroom Learning for Both Users and Nearby Peers," *Computers & Education* 62, (2013): 24–31.

106n students aren't engaged: Evan F. Risko et al., "Everyday Attention: Mind Wandering and Computer Use During Lectures," *Computers & Education* 68, (2013): 275–83.

107 extroverts, for example: Adrian Furnham and Anna Bradley, "Music While You Work: The Differential Distraction of Background Music on the Cognitive Test Performance of Introverts and Extraverts," *Applied Cognitive Psychology* 11, no. 5 (1997): 445–55.

110 the same passage: Laura L. Bowman et al., "Can Students Really Multitask? An Experimental Study of Instant Messaging While Reading," *Computers & Education* 54, no. 4 (2010): 927–31.

CHAPTER 5: MAKING HYPERFOCUS A HABIT

111 trying to focus: Jennifer C. McVay, Michael J. Kane, and Thomas R. Kwapil, "Tracking the Train of Thought from the Laboratory into Everyday Life: An Experience-Sampling Study of Mind Wandering Across Controlled and Ecological Contexts," *Psychonomic Bulletin & Review* 16, no. 5 (2009): 857–63; Paul Seli et al., "Mind-Wandering With and Without Intention," *Trends in Cognitive Sciences* 20, no. 8 (2016): 605–617; Benjamin Baird et al., "Inspired by Distraction: Mind Wandering Facilitates Creative Incubation," *Psychological Science* 23, no. 10 (2012): 1117–22.

112 with such conditions: Gloria Mark, Yiran Wang, and Melissa Niiya, "Stress and Multitasking in Everyday College Life: An Empirical Study of Online Activity," in *Proceedings of the SIGCHI Conference on Human Factors in Computing Systems* (New York: ACM, 2014), 41–50, doi:10.1145/2556288.2557361.

116 like writing reports: Gloria Mark et al., "Bored Mondays and Focused Afternoons: The Rhythm of Attention and Online Activity in the Workplace," in *Proceedings of the SIGCHI Conference on Human Factors in Computing Systems* (New York: ACM, 2014), 3025–34, doi:10.1145/2556288.2557204.

117 on complex tasks: Jennifer C. McVay and Michael J. Kane, "Conducting the Train of Thought: Working Memory Capacity, Goal Neglect, and Mind Wandering in an Executive-Control Task," *Journal of Experimental Psychology: Learning, Memory, and Cognition* 35, no. 1 (2009): 196–204.

117 (and plan for) the future: Benjamin Baird, Jonathan Smallwood, and Jonathan W. Schooler, "Back to the Future: Autobiographical Planning and the Functionality of Mind-Wandering," *Consciousness and Cognition* 20, no. 4 (2011): 1604.

117 "favored mental destination": Ibid.

117 an 85 percent correlation: Klaus Oberauer et al., "Working Memory and Intelligence: Their Correlation and Their Relation: Comment on Ackerman, Beier, and Boyle (2005)," *Psychological Bulletin* 131, no. 1 (2005): 61–65.

117n of job performance: Roberto Colom et al., "Intelligence, Working Memory, and Multitasking Performance," *Intelligence* 38, no. 6 (2010): 543–51.

118 designed to improve!: Adam Hampshire et al., "Putting Brain Training to the Test," *Nature* 465, no. 7299 (2010): 775–78.

119 an average of *16 percent*!: Michael D. Mrazek et al., "Mindfulness Training Improves Working Memory Capacity and GRE Performance While Reducing Mind Wandering," *Psychological Science* 24, no. 5 (2013): 776–81.

119 with personal concerns: Ibid.

119 "of mind wandering": Jonathan Smallwood and Jonathan W. Schooler, "The Science of Mind Wandering: Empirically Navigating the Stream of Consciousness," *Annual Review of Psychology* 66, no. 1 (2015): 487–518.

119 A few weeks: Dianna Quach et al., "A Randomized Controlled Trial Examining the Effect of Mindfulness Meditation on Working Memory Capacity in Adolescents," *Journal of Adolescent Health* 58, no. 5 (2016): 489–96.

122 manage your attention: E. I. de Bruin, J. E. van der Zwan, and S. M. Bogels, "A RCT Comparing Daily Mindfulness Meditations, Biofeedback Exercises, and Daily Physical Exercise on Attention Control, Executive Functioning, Mindful Awareness, Self-Compassion, and Worrying in Stressed Young Adults," *Mindfulness* 7, no. 5 (2016): 1182–92.

125 "Being heard is so close": David W. Augsburger, *Caring Enough to Hear and Be Heard*. (Ventura, CA: Regal Books, 1982).

CHAPTER 6: YOUR BRAIN'S HIDDEN CREATIVE MODE

135 deliberately deploy scatterfocus: J. R. Binder et al., "Conceptual Processing During the Conscious Resting State: A Functional MRI Study," *Journal of Cognitive Neuroscience* 11, no. 1 (1999): 80–93.

135 they were surveyed: Paul Seli, Evan F. Risko, and Daniel Smilek, "On the Necessity of Distinguishing Between Unintentional and Intentional Mind Wandering," *Psychological Science* 27, no. 5 (2016): 685–91.

135 the shock again: University of Virginia, "Doing Something Is Better Than Doing Nothing for Most People, Study Shows," *EurekAlert!*, July 2014.

136 *pleasurable or threatening:* Amit Sood and David T. Jones, "On Mind Wandering, Attention, Brain Networks, and Meditation," *Explore* 9, no. 3 (2013): 136–41.

137 **we wander to the past:** Benjamin Baird, Jonathan Smallwood, and Jonathan W. Schooler, "Back to the Future: Autobiographical Planning and the Functionality of Mind-Wandering," *Consciousness and Cognition* 20, no. 4 (2011).

138 **and the future:** Benjamin Baird, Jonathan Smallwood, and Jonathan W. Schooler, "Back to the Future" Jonathan W. Schooler et al., "Meta-awareness, Perceptual Decoupling and the Wandering Mind," *Trends in Cognitive Sciences* 15, no. 7 (2011): 319–26.

138n **having food stolen:** Sérgio P. C. Correia, Anthony Dickinson, and Nicola S. Clayton, "Western Scrub-jays Anticipate Future Needs Independently of Their Current Motivational State," *Current Biology* 17, no. 10 (2007): 856–61.

138n **rudimentary and limited:** Dan Pink, *When: The Scientific Secrets of Perfect Timing* (New York: Riverhead Books, 2018).

139n **Alzheimer's, and dementia:** Zoran Josipovic et al., "Influence of Meditation on Anti-correlated Networks in the Brain," *Frontiers in Human Neuroscience* 183, no. 5 (2012).

139n **"with average IQ":** Mary Helen Immordino-Yang, Joanna A. Christodoulou, and Vanessa Singh, "Rest Is Not Idleness: Implications of the Brain's Default Mode for Human Development and Education," *Perspectives on Psychological Science* 7, no. 4 (2012): 352–64.

140 **at the same time:** Jonathan Smallwood, interview with the author, November 28, 2017.

140 **is spent planning:** Jessica R. Andrews-Hanna, "The Brain's Default Network and Its Adaptive Role in Internal Mentation," *The Neuroscientist: A Review Journal Bridging Neurobiology, Neurology and Psychiatry* 18, no. 3 (2012): 251; Baird, Smallwood, and Schooler, "Back to the Future."

140 **and more intentionally:** Jonathan Smallwood, Florence J. M. Ruby, and Tania Singer, "Letting Go of the Present: Mind-Wandering Is Associated with Reduced Delay Discounting," *Consciousness and Cognition* 22, no. 1 (2013): 1–7.

141 **future a reality:** Gabriele Oettingen and Bettina Schwörer, "Mind Wandering via Mental Contrasting as a Tool for Behavior Change," *Frontiers in Psychology* 4 (2013): 562.

141 **26 percent of the time:** Baird, Smallwood, and Schooler, "Back to the Future."

141n **stimulating distractions instead:** Smallwood interview.

142 **become more compassionate:** Rebecca L. McMillan, Scott Barry Kaufman, and Jerome L. Singer, "Ode to Positive Constructive Daydreaming," *Frontiers in Psychology* 4 (2013): 626.

148 **think more expansively:** Jonathan Smallwood et al., "Shifting Moods, Wandering Minds: Negative Moods Lead the Mind to Wander," *Emotion* 9, no. 2 (2009): 271–76.

148 **the negative past:** Baird, Smallwood, and Schooler, "Back to the Future."

148 **grows even stronger:** Jonathan Schooler, interview with the author, November 28, 2017; Jonathan Smallwood, Louise Nind, and Rory C. O'Connor, "When Is Your

Head At? An Exploration of the Factors Associated with the Temporal Focus of the Wandering Mind," *Consciousness and Cognition* 18, no. 1 (2009): 118–25.

148 **taking no break whatsoever:** Benjamin W. Mooneyham and Jonathan W. Schooler, "The Costs and Benefits of Mind-Wandering: A Review," *Canadian Journal of Experimental Psychology/Revue canadienne de psychologie expérimentale* 67, no. 1 (2013): 11–18; Benjamin Baird et al., "Inspired by Distraction: Mind Wandering Facilitates Creative Incubation," *Psychological Science* 23, no. 10 (2012): 1117–22.

148 **aware of your thoughts:** Paul Seli et al., "Intrusive Thoughts: Linking Spontaneous Mind Wandering and OCD Symptomatology," *Psychological Research* 81, no. 2 (2017): 392–98.

148 **about the future:** Giorgio Marchetti, "Attention and Working Memory: Two Basic Mechanisms for Constructing Temporal Experiences," *Frontiers in Psychology* 5 (2014): 880.

152 **"possible future events":** Daniel L. Schacter, Randy L. Buckner, and Donna Rose Addis, "Remembering the Past to Imagine the Future: The Prospective Brain," *Nature Reviews Neuroscience* 8, no. 9 (2007): 657–61.

153 **5.4 times every hour:** Schooler et al., "Meta-awareness, Perceptual Decoupling and the Wandering Mind."

153 **"recognizing its occurrence":** Ibid.

CHAPTER 7: RECHARGING YOUR ATTENTION

160 **the same effect:** Kenichi Kuriyama et al., "Sleep Accelerates the Improvement in Working Memory Performance," *Journal of Neuroscience* 28, no. 40 (2008): 10145–50.

161 **you genuinely enjoy:** Jennifer C. McVay, Michael J. Kane, and Thomas R. Kwapil, "Tracking the Train of Thought from the Laboratory into Everyday Life: An Experience-Sampling Study of Mind Wandering Across Controlled and Ecological Contexts," *Psychonomic Bulletin & Review* 16, no. 5 (2009): 857–63; Paul Seli et al., "Increasing Participant Motivation Reduces Rates of Intentional and Unintentional Mind Wandering," *Psychological Research* (2017), doi:10.1007/s00426-017-0914-2.

161 **have three characteristics:** John Trougakos and Ivona Hideg, "Momentary Work Recovery: The Role of Within-Day Work Breaks," in *Current Perspectives on Job-Stress Recovery*, vol. 7, *Research in Occupational Stress and Well-being*, ed. Sabine Sonnentag, Pamela L. Perrewé, and Daniel C. Ganster (West Yorkshire, UK: Emerald Group, 2009).

162 **do resume working:** Ibid.

163 **groups of people:** Sophia Dembling, "Introversion and the Energy Equation," *Psychology Today*, November 2009.

163 **day as well:** Rhymer Rigby, "Open Plan Offices Are Tough on Introverts," *Financial Times*, October 2015.

163n **"gain in income":** Florence Williams, "This Is Your Brain on Nature," *National Geographic*, January 2016.

165 **allow your mind to wander:** Peretz Lavie, Jacob Zomer, and Daniel Gopher, "Ultradian Rhythms in Prolonged Human Performance" (ARI Research Note 95-30, U.S. Army Research Institute for the Behavioral and Social Sciences, 1995).

165 **fifty-two minutes of work:** Julia Gifford, "The Rule of 52 and 17: It's Random, but It Ups Your Productivity," The Muse, no date.

166 **when we're tired:** Kuriyama et al., "Sleep Accelerates the Improvement in Working Memory Performance."

166 **space less often:** James Hamblin, "How to Sleep," *Atlantic*, January 2017.

167 **than it actually is:** Bronwyn Fryer, "Sleep Deficit: The Performance Killer," *Harvard Business Issue*, October 2006; Paula Alhola and Päivi Polo-Kantola, "Sleep Deprivation: Impact on Cognitive Performance," *Neuropsychiatric Disease and Treatment* 3, no. 5 (2007): 553.

167 **stages of sleep:** G. William Domhoff and Kieran C. R. Fox, "Dreaming and the Default Network: A Review, Synthesis, and Counterintuitive Research Proposal," *Consciousness and Cognition* 33 (2015): 342–53.

167 **mode on steroids:** Ibid.

168 **throughout the day:** Gloria Mark et al., "Sleep Debt in Student Life: Online Attention Focus, Facebook, and Mood," in *Proceedings of the Thirty-fourth Annual SIGCHI Conference on Human Factors in Computing Systems* (New York: ACM, 2016), 5517–28, doi:10.1145/2858036.2858437.

168 **midnight, on average:** Gloria Mark, Yiran Wang, and Melissa Niiya, "Stress and Multitasking in Everyday College Life: An Empirical Study of Online Activity," in *Proceedings of the SIGCHI Conference on Human Factors in Computing Systems* (New York: ACM, 2014), 41–50, doi:10.1145/2556288.2557361.

169 **your focus and productivity:** Trougakos and Hideg, "Momentary Work Recovery."

CHAPTER 8: CONNECTING DOTS

172 **encoded into our memory:** J. Gläscher et al., "Distributed Neural System for General Intelligence Revealed by Lesion Mapping," *Proceedings of the National Academy of Sciences of the United States of America* 107, no. 10 (2010): 4705–9.

172n **field of neuroscience:** Randy L. Buckner, "The Serendipitous Discovery of the Brain's Default Network," *Neuroimage* 62, no. 2 (2012): 1137.

173 **study this concept:** E. J. Masicampo and Roy F. Baumeister, "Unfulfilled Goals Interfere with Tasks That Require Executive Functions," *Journal of Experimental Social Psychology* 47, no. 2 (2011): 300–311.

174 **unearth novel solutions:** Jonathan Smallwood and Jonathan W. Schooler, "The Restless Mind," *Psychological Bulletin* 132, no. 6 (2006): 946–58.

175 **number of mistakes:** Ibid.

176 **"on cocktail napkins":** Jonah Lehrer, "The Eureka Hunt," *New Yorker*, July 2008.

179 **in that moment:** S. Dali, *The Secret Life of Salvador Dali* (London: Vision Press, 1976); David Harrison, "Arousal Syndromes: First Functional Unit Revisited," in *Brain Asymmetry and Neural Systems* (Cham, Switzerland: Springer, 2015).

179 **find a solution:** Denise J. Cai et al., "REM, Not Incubation, Improves Creativity by Priming Associative Networks," *Proceedings of the National Academy of Sciences of the United States of America* 106, no. 25 (2009): 10130–34.

179 **dots you encountered:** Carl Zimmer, "The Purpose of Sleep? To Forget, Scientists Say," *New York Times*, February 2017.

180 **you purposefully *un*focus:** Marci S. DeCaro et al., "When Higher Working Memory Capacity Hinders Insight," *Journal of Experimental Psychology: Learning, Memory, and Cognition* 42, no. 1 (2016): 39–49.

180 **through a sentence:** Colleen Seifert et al., "Demystification of Cognitive Insight: Opportunistic Assimilation and the Prepared-Mind Hypothesis," in *The Nature of Insight*, ed. R. Sternberg and J. Davidson (Cambridge, MA: MIT Press, 1994).

CHAPTER 9: COLLECTING DOTS

183 **they're linked together:** Nelson Cowan, "What Are the Differences Between Long-term, Short-term, and Working Memory?" *Progress in Brain Research* 169 (2008): 323–38.

184 **don't consciously retrieve:** Annette Bolte and Thomas Goschke, "Intuition in the Context of Object Perception: Intuitive Gestalt Judgments Rest on the Unconscious Activation of Semantic Representations," *Cognition* 108, no. 3 (2008): 608–16.

187 **supports what you know:** Elizabeth Kolbert, "Why Facts Don't Change Our Minds," *New Yorker*, February 2017.

191 **more useful pursuits:** "The Cross-Platform Report: A New Connected Community," *Nielsen*, November 2012.

195 **writer Arthur C. Clarke:** "Hazards of Prophecy: The Failure of Imagination," in *Profiles of the Future: An Enquiry into the Limits of the Possible* (New York: Harper & Row, 1962, rev. 1973), 14, 21, 36.

196 **Malcolm Gladwell wrote:** Malcolm Gladwell, *Outliers: The Story of Success*, (New York: Little, Brown and Co., 2008).

196 **connections others hadn't:** Walter Isaacson, *Einstein: His Life and Universe* (New York: Simon & Schuster, 2008), 352.

196 **"only passionately curious":** Isaacson, *Einstein*, 548.

196 **theory of relativity:** Ibid.

196 **"in prison yet":** Ibid., 307.

196 **"how much Mozart practiced":** Daniel Levitin, *This Is Your Brain on Music: The Science of a Human Obsession* (New York: Dutton, 2008).

196n **came to him:** Nick Mojica, "Lin-Manuel Miranda Freestyles Off the Dome During 5 Fingers of Death," *XXL Mag*, October 2017.

198 **between hyperfocus and scatterfocus:** John Kounios, *The Eureka Factor: Aha Moments, Creative Insight, and the Brain* (New York: Random House, 2015), 208.

CHAPTER 10: WORKING TOGETHER

201 **In one study:** Gabriele Oettingen and Bettina Schwörer, "Mind Wandering via Mental Contrasting as a Tool for Behavior Change," *Frontiers in Psychology* 4 (2013): 562; Gabriele Oettingen, "Future Thought and Behaviour Change," *European Review of Social Psychology* 23, no. 1 (2012): 1–63.

202 **on something mundane:** Matthew A. Killingsworth and Daniel T. Gilbert, "A Wandering Mind Is an Unhappy Mind," *Science* 330, no. 6006 (2010): 932.

202 **experience all three:** Michael S. Franklin et al., "The Silver Lining of a Mind in the Clouds: Interesting Musings Are Associated with Positive Mood While Mind-Wandering," *Frontiers in Psychology* 4 (2013): 583.

202 **mode you're in:** Jonathan Smallwood et al., "Shifting Moods, Wandering Minds: Negative Moods Lead the Mind to Wander," *Emotion* 9, no. 2 (2009): 271–76.

202 **and accomplish more:** F. Gregory Ashby, Alice M. Isen, and And U. Turken, "A Neuropsychological Theory of Positive Affect and Its Influence on Cognition," *Psychological Review* 106, no. 3 (1999): 529–50.

202 **the risky kind:** Ibid.

202 **front of you:** Jonathan Smallwood and Jonathan W. Schooler, "The Science of Mind Wandering: Empirically Navigating the Stream of Consciousness," *Annual Review of Psychology* 66, no. 1 (2015): 487–518.

203 **took place then:** Jonathan Smallwood and Rory C. O'Connor, "Imprisoned by the Past: Unhappy Moods Lead to a Retrospective Bias to Mind Wandering," *Cognition & Emotion* 25, no. 8 (2011): 1481–90.

203 **think of them more:** Jonathan W. Schooler, interview with the author, November 28, 2017.

203 **"recovering depressive individuals":** Jonathan Smallwood and Jonathan W. Schooler, "The Restless Mind," *Psychological Bulletin* 132, no. 6 (2006): 946–58.

203 **negative or neutral state:** Shawn Achor, *The Happiness Advantage: The Seven Principles of Positive Psychology That Fuel Success and Performance at Work* (New York: Currency, 2010).

203 **which to work:** Karuna Subramaniam et al., "A Brain Mechanism for Facilitation of Insight by Positive Affect," *Journal of Cognitive Neuroscience* 21, no. 3 (2009): 415–32.

204 **thousands of subjects:** Killingsworth and Gilbert, "A Wandering Mind Is an Unhappy Mind."

204 **bolster your happiness:** Shawn Achor, "The Happy Secret to Better Work," TED .com, 2011, www.ted.com/talks/shawn_achor_the_happy_secret_to_better_work.

206 **number of ideas:** Mareike B. Wieth and Rose T. Zacks, "Time of Day Effects on Problem Solving: When the Non-optimal Is Optimal," *Thinking & Reasoning* 17, no. 4 (2011): 387–401.

206 **naturally more tired:** Ibid.

206 **engaged on Fridays:** Gloria Mark et al., "Bored Mondays and Focused Afternoons: The Rhythm of Attention and Online Activity in the Workplace," in *Proceedings of the SIGCHI Conference on Human Factors in Computing Systems* (New York: ACM, 2014), 3025–34, doi:10.1145/2556288.2557204.

207 **drinks in the process:** Andrew F. Jarosz et al., "Uncorking the Muse: Alcohol Intoxication Facilitates Creative Problem Solving," *Consciousness and Cognition* 21, no. 1 (2012): 487–93.

208 **mind has wandered:** Michael A. Sayette, Erik D. Reichle, and Jonathan W. Schooler, "Lost in the Sauce: The Effects of Alcohol on Mind Wandering," *Psychological Science* 20, no. 6 (2009): 747–52.

208 **pretty much anything:** Jarosz, Colflesh, and Wiley. "Uncorking the Muse."

209 **a jigsaw puzzle:** Tom M. McLellan, John A. Caldwell, and Harris R. Lieberman, "A Review of Caffeine's Effects on Cognitive, Physical and Occupational Performance," *Neuroscience & Biobehavioral Reviews* 71 (2016): 294–312.

209 **performance becomes impaired:** Ibid.

210 **often as well:** Laura Dabbish, Gloria Mark, and Victor González, "Why Do I Keep Interrupting Myself? Environment, Habit and Self-Interruption," in *Proceedings of the SIGCHI Conference on Human Factors in Computing Systems* (New York: ACM, 2011), 3127–30, doi:10.1145/1978942.1979405; Gloria Mark, Victor Gonzalez, and Justin Harris, "No Task Left Behind? Examining the Nature of Fragmented Work," *Proceedings of the SIGCHI Conference on Human Factors in Computing Systems* (New York: ACM, 2005), 321–30, doi:10.1145/1054972.1055017.

210n **in your mouth:** McLellan et al., "A Review of Caffeine's Effect."

211 **energy to refocus:** Mark, Gonzalez, and Harris, "No Task Left Behind?"

211 **fell by 30 percent:** R. van Solingen, E. Berghout, and F. van Latum, "Interrupts: Just a Minute Never Is," *IEEE Software* 15, no. 5 (1998): 97–103; Edward R. Sykes, "Interruptions in the Workplace: A Case Study to Reduce Their Effects," *International Journal of Information Management* 31, no. 4 (2011): 385–94.

212 **and less costly:** van Solingen, Berghout, and van Latum, "Interrupts."

213 **hyperfocus or scatterfocus accordingly:** Claire M. Zedelius and Jonathan W. Schooler, "Mind Wandering 'Ahas' Versus Mindful Reasoning: Alternative Routes to Creative Solutions," *Frontiers in Psychology* 6 (2015): 834.

INDEX